W9-BMR-122

CLOSING THE OPPORTUNITY GAP

CLOSING THE OPPORTUNITY GAP

Identity-Conscious Strategies for Retention and Student Success

Edited by Vijay Pendakur

Foreword by Shaun R. Harper

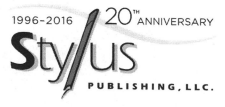

1996–2016 20TH ANNIVERSARY

Stylus

PUBLISHING, LLC.

STERLING, VIRGINIA

COPYRIGHT © 2016 BY STYLUS
PUBLISHING, LLC.

Published by Stylus Publishing, LLC.
22883 Quicksilver Drive
Sterling, Virginia 20166-2102

All rights reserved. No part of this book may be reprinted or
reproduced in any form or by any electronic, mechanical, or other
means, now known or hereafter invented, including photocopying,
recording, and information storage and retrieval, without
permission in writing from the publisher.

Library of Congress Cataloging-in-Publication Data
Names: Pendakur, Vijay, editor of compilation.
Title: Closing the opportunity gap : identity-conscious strategies for
retention and student success / edited by Vijay Pendakur ; foreword
by Shaun R. Harper.
Description: First edition. |
Sterling, Virginia : Stylus Publishing, 2016 |
Includes bibliographical references and index.
Identifiers: LCCN 2015036544|
    ISBN 9781620363119 (cloth : alk. paper) |
    ISBN 9781620363126 (pbk. : alk. paper) |
    ISBN 9781620363133 (library networkable e-edition) |
    ISBN 9781620363140 (consumer e-edition)
Subjects: LCSH: College dropouts--Prevention. |
Minority college students. | First-generation college students. |
Educational equalization. | Culturally relevant pedagogy.
Classification: LCC LC148.15 .C55 2016 | DDC 378.1/6913–
dc23 LC record available at http://lccn.loc.gov/2015036544

13-digit ISBN: 978-1-62036-311-9 (cloth)
13-digit ISBN: 978-1-62036-312-6 (paperback)
13-digit ISBN: 978-1-62036-313-3 (library networkable e-edition)
13-digit ISBN: 978-1-62036-314-0 (consumer e-edition)

Printed in the United States of America

All first editions printed on acid-free paper
that meets the American National Standards Institute
Z39-48 Standard.

Bulk Purchases

Quantity discounts are available for use in workshops and for
staff development.
Call 1-800-232-0223

First Edition, 2016

10   9   8   7   6   5   4   3   2   1

To Katie . . . there's no place I'd rather be.

CONTENTS

FOREWORD

Truth is, many populations have long been systematically denied opportunities to succeed at colleges and universities in the United States. The opportunity gap was not born overnight; it is not a recent phenomenon. For some groups, it starts before they are born and follows them from preschool through postsecondary education. In most instances, these people and their families do not voluntarily place themselves on lower ends of social, educational, and economic trend lines. While assorted metrics are routinely used to measure, document, and make sense of statistical differences in student progress and performance, it is important to note that the disparities themselves have little to do with students' abilities to achieve. The *achievement gap*, as it is commonly called, connotes that some groups more strongly prefer or perhaps are more genetically predisposed to succeed than others. It tends to be decontextualized, masking the structural racism, sexism, and classism that cyclically reproduce inequities in education and society.

Conversations about the so-called achievement gap tend to blame those who are persistently underserved for their bad academic performance outcomes. Such discourse could lead someone to erroneously conclude that certain groups, their families, and their communities, for one reason or another, deliberately refuse to succeed—that students from low-income families, for example, actually want to live in poverty for the rest of their lives. I know these people. They are my people. I was once one of them. In many ways, I will always be one of them. Hence, I know for sure that we want better; we deserve fairness; and we would achieve at much higher rates were there fewer political, economic, and educational barriers to our success. In this way, it is not about an achievement gap; rather, it is about the inequitable distribution of opportunities. Vijay Pendakur and the contributors to this book clearly understand this.

Too little attention has been devoted to the opportunity gap in higher education. There is countless statistical documentation of inequities among groups seeking access to and success in college, but, for some reason, such disparities are not often viewed as opportunity gaps. This book is an extraordinary contribution to the literature on student success in higher education because it necessarily complicates conversations about college opportunity. It gives us language to critically engage in the shift in discourse and accountability work its editor calls for in the introduction. To further contextualize the important perspectives and recommendations presented in this text, I offer three additional sets of insights on the opportunity gap in U.S. higher education.

Historical Determinants of Success

Several groups have been categorically excluded from particular sectors of higher education far longer than they have been allowed to enroll. Meanwhile, privileged others amassed various forms of capital on college and university campuses that have been transmitted and expended by generations of their family members and others who share similar demographic and social characteristics (male, White, wealthy, Christian, heterosexual, etc.). Given this, students of color and their low-income peers are continually behind in a race in which others benefit from a multigenerational head start. They face the challenge of trying to make institutions not built for them adapt to their needs and expectations; redress long-standing cultural and curricular assaults on their humanity; and afford them equitable access to resources that will ultimately enable them to thrive personally, educationally, and professionally. Inequities are firmly etched into the architecture and functioning of most institutions, a reality that is not often sufficiently considered when making sense of why some groups succeed at rates much higher than others.

Throughout the lifespan of U.S. higher education, opportunity has also been stratified by institution type. The opportunity gap has always privileged predominantly White institutions, especially those with large endowments, state-of-the-art laboratories and other facilities, and politically powerful supporters in state legislatures and governors' offices. The gap has been most unkind to historically Black colleges and universities, community colleges, and other institutions that offer the greatest access to the most underserved citizens (those who attended under-resourced P–12 public schools, Pell Grant recipients, returning adult learners, and first-generation college goers, to name a few). In most states, these schools have never really been afforded their fair share of resources to create the conditions necessary to ensure success for more students. Without serious commitments to understanding and strategically redressing historical inequities within and among institutions, the opportunity gap will continue to be persistent and pervasive.

Structural Forces and Agents for Student Success

Estela Mara Bensimon—my dear friend and colleague whose work is generously cited in chapter 7 of this book—and I often teach, speak, and write about the important role of institutional agents in student success. It frustrates her and me that traditional, widely cited theories in higher education disproportionately (sometimes entirely) place the onus for student success on students themselves. For instance, there has been a long-standing fascination with student effort and engagement—how students spend their time and the corresponding outcomes associated with their participation in those activities and experiences. Not enough emphasis is placed on what postsecondary educators do to engage students. Institutional agents play a serious role in sustaining structural barriers to opportunity for particular groups. They do so through their investment in maintaining curricula, pedagogies, and programmatic approaches that were created for a considerably less diverse student population. They also do so through colorblind, class-neutral commitments to doing the same thing for every student.

Professor Bensimon and I have long contended that students do not have equitable opportunities to succeed if institutional agents do not strategically embed equity into educational policies and practices. Equality is doing the same thing for everyone, despite their unique needs and experiences on campuses not built for them; interactions with systems that repeatedly advantage their more privileged peers; and enrollment in classes taught by faculty who stereotype them and refuse to thoughtfully integrate non-Eurocentric, non-upper-income perspectives into readings and class discussions. The opportunity gap is a byproduct of structural disadvantage and disregard, not a result of students' unwillingness to be successful. The identity consciousness and identity centeredness emphasized throughout this book demand that institutional agents assume greater responsibility for equity and student success.

Deficit Views of Underserved Populations

Undoubtedly, the opportunity gap is sustained and exacerbated by the ways in which institutional agents have been socialized to view particular groups of students as troubled, underprepared, unmotivated, anti-intellectual, and dangerous. Stereotypes about undocumented students, Native Americans, low-income Whites, and others influence how much professors invest in them, believe they can do academically, and expect of them. I once heard Vincent Tinto say, "No student rises to low expectations." Sadly, those who are most harmed by the opportunity gap are forced to succeed despite the low expectations institutional agents convey to them and others like them.

Moreover, I have been saying for 12 years now that anyone who is serious about improving rates of success for particular groups (e.g., Black and Latino undergraduate men) have much to learn from persons in the group who have succeeded, despite the odds stacked against them. Educators, even the most committed among us, cannot close the opportunity gap without doing more of what works to bolster achievement among the most persistently under-served students. We can actualize the imperative that Pendakur articulates in this book if we seize opportunities to right past wrongs, address systemic institutional threats to achievement, and learn from the success that is often hiding in plain sight. This book will help us.

Shaun R. Harper
Philadelphia, Pennsylvania

ACKNOWLEDGMENTS

As an editor, a.k.a. chief convener and cajoler, I have been blessed with an amazing group of contributors to this project. I'd like to start with a big thank-you to the entire group for their brilliance and hard work on these chapters as well as their transformative engagement with students. The majority trace back to the Office of Multicultural Student Success at DePaul University, and I wouldn't be who I am today if it weren't for the community we formed and everyone's willingness to be unfailingly creative and generous in developing the approach that is at the heart of this book.

Much love and gratitude to my mom and dad for their continual interest in all aspects of my life, including this book. I appreciate how much of an investment they have in growing with me. Sumi, you and I have spoken about this book since that fateful SASpeaks at NASPA where you geeked out and took pictures of me by crawling into the aisle. Thanks for being an amazing big sis, always.

Art and Ann Marie, I can't tell you how lucky I am to have you as friends, confidants, and colleagues. Thanks for picking up the phone and talking me off the ledge. More of that to come! Kevin and Karu, your willingness to participate in our annual conference meet-up ritual is a source of much inspiration and revitalization for me. A book project is a long haul, and I wouldn't have enjoyed the process as much without your companionship.

Teri, your willingness to invest immensely in me continues to surprise me, and I should just accept this truth by now: You are the craftiest, most generous, hilarious, and loyal friend. I can't wait until our next adventure together.

To Rico, for always asking, What does success look like? To Lea, for instantly becoming my homie. Between you two, this book project was offered the space to begin and the support to finish.

To Jennifer, for your eagle eye and committed heart. It's not frequent to find an editorial companion that cares so deeply about the content of a book, or the students at the heart of a project.

And last, but not least, to CB4, Guf, Bri, Vega Obscura, Seanie Dee, Marty, Byron, EJ, and LeKoop for giving me the gift of being understood. The world would be a lonely place for me without your friendship.

INTRODUCTION
Two Distinct Paths and a Missed Opportunity

Vijay Pendakur

When I was in my late 20s, a good friend urged me to use my skill and experience as a diversity educator to form a consulting business in addition to working as a full-time student affairs professional. While at first this sounded like a recipe for taking on too much work, it turned out to be one of the most enjoyable side endeavors of my adult life. I had the privilege of being invited to speak on dozens of campuses around the country, from small, elite liberal arts colleges to large research universities. In my first year as a speaker, I found it curious that the majority of the officials who hired me wanted to give me a campus tour. In time, however, I realized that this practice falls under a mix of good hosting techniques and campus pride for many institutions, so I began to relax and look forward to these tours. After all, as a lifetime higher education professional, how could I pass on the chance to collect data on campuses around the country?

As the number of speaking engagements continued to grow, I began to notice a pattern in my informal data collection experience. The campuses I visited generally seemed to have some investment in academic retention and student success, which included finishing 30 credits in the first year, four-year graduation campaigns, new technology platforms that enable academic advisers to better engage at-risk students, early-alert systems, learning management systems to help students in their activities outside the classroom, freshmen interest groups by academic discipline, or academic advising centers that conduct intrusive advising for probationary students. These programs were generally spread throughout the institution among units and departments in academic affairs, student affairs, and enrollment management.

Most of the campuses I visited also had some investment in spaces or programs focused on diversity and cultural enrichment. These programs or departments, such as multicultural student affairs offices or identity-based

1

student centers, engaged students in curricular and cocurricular efforts to deepen their understanding of their own and others' identities to promote a more inclusive and equitable campus environment. Some campuses even offered equity and inclusion centers that specifically focused on privileged group members' identities in an effort to create a campus conversation on White privilege, patriarchy, or heteronormativity.[1]

As I continued to work as a facilitator and speaker on campuses across the country, my full-time job as a student affairs professional began to change as well. In 2008 I was working as the director of a relatively traditional identity- and culture-focused multicultural student affairs department at DePaul University that was suddenly tasked with shifting its focus toward student persistence and graduation programming. I worked with an amazing team of student affairs educators to create a new model of engaging students, incorporate nuanced data into our understanding of risk and success, and develop robust partnerships with enrollment management and academic affairs to create streamlined pathways for higher-risk students to pursue timely graduation. Having existed for years as an identity- and culture-focused staff, however, we were reluctant to leave our roots behind. We organically developed an intersectional model that incorporated the strategies and outcomes of student success work into an identity-conscious program design framework, and the results were extraordinary. My years as director of DePaul's Office of Multicultural Student Success propelled me into my current role as the associate vice president for student retention at California State University, Fullerton. At this large, access-focused, public institution, I work with an equally amazing team to shape the university itself to promote student success rather than focusing on individual programs and initiatives.

My journey, which started with consulting on dozens of campuses, progressed to changing the course of a department and now involves transforming the shape of a university, has taught me that an intersectional approach is critical if we are going to serve our students effectively. While academic retention efforts and identity development programs are powerful forces that shape the student experience, campus administrators often seem to be missing a key set of strategies that come from the intersection of these two fields. In the current model, students are either being engaged through retention efforts in an identity-neutral framework or in diversity and cultural spaces in an identity-centered framework. This approach often underserves students who are at risk for not making adequate academic progress because of the identities they carry and how these identities shape the way they experience a campus.

Let me bring this problem to life through a hypothetical example: fresh-men orientation, an intervention that has come to be seen as a key retention investment. Imagine a well-designed, two-day summer orientation program at an institution whose administrators understand the connection between strong onboarding and strong student persistence in the first year. Now, imagine Christina, a first-generation Latina student, attending this orienta-tion program with her parents, who possess only limited English capabilities. If the orientation program is designed using an identity-neutral framework, its one-size-fits-all model might run the risk of deeply underserving Christina and her family. For example, an identity-neutral two-day orientation might not have any breakout sessions for first-generation families, where deeper conversations can take place among university representatives, families, and students about the shifting nature of moving from high school to college and the level of family support necessary to foster success in this next phase of life. If Christina's parents assume that college will be just like high school, then their expectations might limit Christina's ability to pursue a leadership position on campus or to study abroad at some point during her undergradu-ate years. Furthermore, an identity-neutral orientation might underserve stu-dents of color by not offering any engagement that prepares them to enter a predominantly White institutional culture. Special sessions that involve students of color and their families in college readiness practices, such as asking professors for help early and often, taking advantage of the campus multicultural center, and finding a mentor in freshmen year, could make a huge difference in Christina's positive first-year experience and her abil-ity to maintain a high grade point average (GPA) and complete the correct amount of credits. Again, an identity-neutral orientation program would not offer these additional sessions. It's not that campuses are without the cross-cultural knowledge to offer intersectional, identity-conscious student success programs, but rather the expertise on students of color and first-generation students is often compartmentalized in diversity units that are not considered part of the retention and student success architecture and, therefore, are not included in the design of orientation programs from the ground up.

In the nearly 10 years I've been visiting campuses around the country, I've seen a steady growing interest in student success and meaningful diver-sity engagement. Yet, I also continue to see these two key investments lie in silos at most institutions, resulting in identity-neutral retention efforts and compartmentalized cultural enrichment programs. These two distinct paths are a missed opportunity and a crisis as our nation faces a growing opportunity gap between students of color and low-income students and their more privileged peers. In this book I contend that an intersectional, identity-conscious approach to retention and student success is the missing ingredient in the national movement to not simply admit a more diverse group of students into higher education but to support these students so they can thrive and graduate on time. The next section of this introduction contextualizes the student success landscape of higher education, specifically focusing on the opportunity gap, before concluding with a clear discussion of what identity-conscious practices are and their potential to revolutionize our efforts.

Closing the Opportunity Gap: A National Imperative

If you've been reading the newspapers, blogs, and trade magazines on higher education in the new millennium, you've probably noticed a growing, intense focus on college completion. After several decades of asking, Who's going to college? we have begun to ask, Who's succeeding in college? The answers are often shocking and disturbing. Only half of our nation's college students who attempt obtaining a bachelor's degree end up completing one within six years of starting. Even more distressing are the numbers from the community college sector, with less than a third of our students obtaining a credential within three years of starting (Brusi, Cruz, Engle, & Yeado, 2012). When taken as a whole, these facts shake the core of the cliché that college is the best four years of your life. To be less tongue in cheek, the statistics turn back the mirror of accountability on higher education and challenge us to start making dramatic, transformative shifts in the way we engage students so they can be more successful in community college and baccalaureate-granting institutions.

Thankfully, higher education leaders have not been passively watching our students fall behind. In response to the national conversation on student success, leaders from a number of colleges and universities came together in 2007 to design a national effort to accomplish two goals: increase the total number of college graduates in the country and ensure that the diversity of those graduates more accurately reflects the current demographics of the country's high school graduates. They branded this national campaign the Access to Success (A2S) Initiative, received support from the Bill & Melinda Gates Foundation and the Lumina Foundation, and invited their fellow college and university leaders to join the campaign. These leaders pledged that "by 2015 . . . their systems will halve the gaps in college-going and college success that separate African-American, Latino, and American-Indian students from white and Asian-American students—and low-income students from more affluent students" (Engle & Lynch, 2009). Soon after the beginning of this effort, 312 two-year and four-year institutions had joined the movement to focus on outcomes and not just admission. Today, 22 multicampus university systems are represented in the A2S initiative, with more than 3.5 million students attending these institutions (Brusi et al., 2012). The A2S initiative is the largest concentrated effort to change the outcomes of higher education, now representing one in five students attending institutions of higher education in the United States (Brusi et al., 2012).

According to the A2S midterm report, there have been tremendous gains on the access goals of the initiative, and, as a result, students of color and low-income students are being admitted to a variety of institutions at greater rates than before the initiative was launched (Brusi et al., 2012). When examining the student success goals, however, a number of gaps remain in the achievement patterns of various student groups. For example, only one in five underreppresented freshmen in community colleges earn a certificate or associate's degree, compared to one in three of their peers (Brusi et al., 2012).[2] In baccalaureate-granting institutions, underrepresented minorities are 16% less likely than their peers to earn a degree within six years (Brusi et al., 2012). Low-income students also face achievement gaps at community colleges and baccalaureate-granting institutions across the country.

One extremely provocative finding of the midterm report is that underrepresented minorities and low-income students have actually experienced success gains at all institution types—but their gains have not kept pace with those of their peers (Brusi et al., 2012). For example, if an institution manages to improve its overall success metrics by 10%, but underrepresented minorities and low-income students were previously behind by 14%, then even after everyone improves by 10%, the 14% gap still remains firmly intact. The A2S midterm report states,

> It is important to note, however, that more than 60 percent of systems have improved graduation rates for underrepresented minorities and more than 40 percent have done so for low-income students. . . . Success gaps have remained stubborn not because success rates have not improved for underrepresented students, but rather because they have not improved fast enough relative to their peers. (p. 13)

To close the opportunity gap, institutions must invest in strategies and programs that are specifically designed to promote student success in the populations that are lagging behind.

Taken as a whole, the A2S initiative is the best study we have of the current terrain of risk and success in higher education. The results from the midterm report (Brusi et al., 2012) demonstrate that the challenge facing us

Shifting the Discourse: From Achievement to Opportunity

Although much of the national discourse frames the gap problem as an achievement gap, I prefer to join the growing trend to focus on the opportunity gap instead. This is not simply a semantic shift but a strategic attempt to shift the locus of the problem from individual students and their collegiate achievement to institutions of higher education and their administrators' willingness to capitalize on the enormous opportunity they have to empower every student they admit to thrive in college and to graduate in a timely manner. A narrow focus on student achievement comes at the exclusion of questions of institutional responsibility to address policy, systems, and environmental factors that contribute to student achievement or failure. Because campus admissions criteria are supposed to be linked to a student's ability to succeed within the rigor of a specific curricular environment, every admitted student should have the opportunity to become engaged on campus; make meaningful connections with faculty, staff, and peers; and graduate ready for postbaccalaureate life. The opportunity gap represents the reality that higher education is currently structured in a way that produces significantly lower outcomes for students of color, low-income college students, and first-generation students.

is in closing the opportunity gap for students of color, low-income students, and first-generation college students. However, to do this, we are going to need a different playbook from the standard retention and student success manual colleges and universities appear to be using today.

Identity-Conscious Approaches: The Missing Ingredient

I began this introduction with a reflection on the current landscape of retention and identity investments at most colleges and universities: identity-neutral, campuswide retention efforts that are distinct and separate from identity-centered diversity and cultural enrichment programs. These two parallel paths represent a missed opportunity to take the depth of knowledge and skill from diversity and cultural programs and employ them in a retention and student success ethos. We must provide students of color, low-income students, and first-generation college students with retention and success services and programs that are designed with their identities in mind.

The foundational philosophy of this book is that programs and services have to begin with a clear picture of who they are trying to serve before the curriculum or plan is developed. If an identity-neutral framework is employed in the program design, then students whose identities are inextricably tied to their risk will be underserved by these efforts. Consider the orientation example from the start of this introduction. Christina's Latina identity and her first-generation status are at the heart of how she experiences orientation. An identity-neutral orientation that ignores Christina's key components will not serve as a student success mechanism for her onboarding and first-year experience. Rather, Christina and her family might actually leave orientation feeling overwhelmed, insecure, and underprepared for making a successful transition to college. The findings of the A2S midterm report (Brusi et al., 2012) support this philosophy as the vast majority of the efforts under way at member institutions are identity-neutral in nature, and the resulting gains for privileged students have outpaced the gains for marginalized students.

In developing the foundational philosophy of this book, I found myself interacting with numerous colleagues throughout the country who work in diversity and cultural centers whose administrators have struggled to understand the difference between what they already do and this alternative framework of identity consciousness. To offer some clarity, I've termed the basic pedagogy and curricula of diversity and cultural centers *identity centered* to distinguish it from identity-conscious pedagogy, curricula, strategy, or practice. Identity consciousness is not the same thing as identity-centered engagement. In an identity-centered program or curriculum, the identity itself is the focus of the intervention. For example, a Latino men's program can be developed as an identity-centered initiative if the outcomes of the program are all tied to a deeper or more complex understanding of one's Latino-ness or masculinity. Alternatively, this same program can be an identity-conscious student success program if it is designed from the ground up with the students' racial and gender identities in mind, but the intended outcomes are tied to student success, such as term-to-term credit completion, yearly persistence, engagement in high-impact practices, or timely graduation. The identity-conscious student success program for Latino men might start with what appears to be a traditional diversity or cultural engagement curriculum, but this only establishes a foundation for further dialogue and skill building tied to retention and student success.

Although the difference between identity consciousness and identity centeredness might appear to be semantic on the surface, it can manifest itself in a profound way when examining outcomes. Identity-centered initiatives in cultural centers can often be considered successful if the right number of students are involved in the program, if they gain a greater appreciation for their cultural identity as well as other concepts of power and privilege, and if key learning outcomes are met. The success metrics for an identity-conscious retention or student success program must be tied to institutional success metrics, such as yearly persistence, high-performance GPA groupings, or timely graduation rates. These markedly different outcomes demand appropriately different uses of time and energy in a student-focused program.

How to Use This Book

This book is for higher education professionals in every arena of the academy: student affairs educators, faculty, and staff in academic affairs or enrollment management units. It is intended to be a practical how-to manual for higher education professionals who are interested in closing the opportunity gap at their institutions. Each chapter offers a different identity-conscious student success curriculum or strategy, such as parent programs for students of color and low-income students, women of color leadership development curricula, and hunger and homelessness initiatives for low-income students. In the spirit of applicability, the contributing authors focus their chapters on usable program development guides rather than lengthy reviews of the literature or research. There is a rich scholarly tradition on college students, retention, and identity development. This book is intentionally focused on the how-to practicality of program implementation to respond to the crisis higher education is facing rather than on research and theory. It is our hope that you'll find this book inspirational and pragmatic and that reading it will provoke you to take action and create change.

This edited volume can be read as a whole, cover to cover, or if you are a higher education professional with an immediate need, you can flip to a chapter to access information about a specific population or curriculum. Because higher education is a very diverse landscape, these chapters are designed for professionals at community colleges, access-focused comprehensive universities, research-focused universities, and small liberal arts institutions. Often retention and student success efforts are considered irrelevant at elite, highly selective institutions that often have 95% four-year graduation rates. However, this book is particularly useful in these contexts as students of color, low-income students, and first-generation students often face numerous psychosocial risks that can dampen their engagement in, and enjoyment of, the college experience at elite institutions. The strategies and programs in this book can help students at elite institutions not just survive but thrive in higher education.

This book is also meant to help you take action on your campus, and each chapter ends with a list of action items that you can follow to launch a particular strategy in your community. In an effort to establish a sustained dialogue on identity consciousness, student success, and closing the opportunity gap, we've also provided contributor biographies at the end of this book, and we urge you to connect with them to begin a partnership for equity and change.

I hope you enjoy reading these chapters as much as I've loved collaborating with the passionate, skilled group of higher education professionals who wrote them. Let's work together to ensure that the next century of American higher education is a century of success for all our students.

Notes

1.Throughout this introduction, I use *privileged* student or group member for individuals who carry identities that confer unearned advantages on them in the collegiate experience, such as Whites, wealthy people, or students whose parents have baccalaureate degrees from U.S. institutions.

2. A2S uses the term *underrepresented* to indicate Black and Latino students as well as low-income students. The issue of numerical representation as a measure of risk is complex and highly debated, as this framework frequently omits Asian American and Pacific Islander students from the analysis. While we are firmly committed to the inclusion in this book of Asian American and Pacific Islander students as students of color and students who face unique risks in the White institutional culture, the methodology of the A2S limits its focus to Black and Latino students as well as low-income White students.

References

Brusi, R., Cruz, J. L., Engle, J., & Yeado, J. (2012). *Replenishing opportunity in America: The 2012 midterm report of public higher education systems in the Access to Success Initiative*. Washington, DC: Education Trust.

Engle, J., & Lynch, M. (2009). *Charting a necessary path: A baseline report of the Access to Success Initiative*. Washington, DC: Education Trust.

FAMILY ENGAGEMENT FOR FIRST-GENERATION FAMILIES AND FAMILIES OF COLOR

Andrea Arzuaga

Last fall, first-year student Doria (not her real name) came into my office in tears. She came from class, a required biology course for her major, where she learned that she failed another exam. As was the case with the previous exam, Doria had not been able to devote a lot of time to studying because she had an off-campus job and needed to work at least 30 hours a week to help supplement her family's income. When we started to talk about her devoting more time to course work and studying, she said that while in high school she could work the same amount of hours and get great grades but that college course work was proving more difficult. I asked if she and her family had discussed cutting her hours at work and perhaps contributing less as a short-term solution for her to complete her degree and have more earning power in the long run. She said her parents would never understand and had told her she simply needed to work harder. She was the first in her family to attend college, and she felt that her family did not understand the rigors of college. We spent the next few weeks looking for on-campus positions that would allow Doria more time for study while still making money, but she still struggled for the rest of the quarter and wound up needing to cut back on her credit hours for the next term to save money and try to get better grades.

Each year, students like Doria come to my office with what feels like the worst problem in the world; they have an issue and are unsure or afraid of how to talk to their families about it. Sometimes this issue is financial; sometimes it's academic; and sometimes it's about balancing their life as a student, part-time employee, and family member. In each case, however, a critical intervention would have stopped the issue from ever becoming a crisis, such as a chance for students to discuss with family members their values and expectations during the college transition and orientation process. Without this communication, families are often unable to provide the support we know is integral to student persistence and student success. This chapter discusses the ways parents and families of first-generation college students and students of color can be involved and empowered, in person and electronically, so they can more effectively contribute to the success of their students.

Overview

The parents and families of first-generation college students and students of color are a resource not always used to help make a positive impact on students' success. Providing programming and resources for these families empowers them to support these students, despite the fact that they have historically been left out of opportunities in which to participate and that would help them better understand higher education. This chapter underscores the historic role parents and families have played in students' lives and addresses the unique needs of first-generation college students and students of color and their families. It concludes with an overview of successful strategies for involving these populations, followed by actionable steps for implementing them across an institution.

Chapter Framework

The extent of parents' and families' involvement has played a significant role in their children's education and has varied throughout the history of higher education in America. The idea of the university as a parent, in loco parentis, was prevalent in the nineteenth century as colleges implemented rules regarding curfew, dress, and varying policies that addressed student behaviors (Donovan & McKelfresh, 2008). Since then, the roles and responsibilities of student affairs professionals have gone through numerous transformations. Administrators have taken varied approaches, from being spectators in their students' experiences to serving as a safety net (Donovan & McKelfresh, 2008). Modern higher education professionals have come to embrace their dual role of educator and advocate for student success in varying degrees of interaction with students' families.

In the twenty-first century, many families are eager to be involved in their children's education from primary and secondary school to the college experience. Involved parents enjoy the parenting role they have maintained over their child's lifetime until college and have no desire to step back (Jacobson, 2003). The needs of these helicopter parents have been met with increased programmatic efforts from universities, including orientation sessions, family weekends, and online portals, and for good reason: Students with involved parents, even when controlling for level of education among family members, do better in areas such as grade point average, credit hours earned, and overall engagement than their peers with less involved parents (Mathews, 2007). Although engagement programs take into account the families who are knowledgeable about college-going processes and have the ability to connect with their child's college through multiple outlets, they are not always effective in involving the families of first-generation college students or students of color. For many of these families, the college-going experience is new and unfamiliar, which can make it difficult for them to help their children make the transition to college life.

Parents who have achieved a high level of education and high socioeconomic status build enough social and cultural capital to understand the college experience (Donovan & McKelfresh, 2008). They use the information they have personally gathered about the college experience and become more involved in their children's higher education. As studies show, this increases students' ability to understand the college experience and overcome obstacles to succeed (Donovan and McKelfresh, 2008). However, marginalized parents and families have not achieved the social and cultural capital needed to be involved in their children's higher education at the same level as their White college-educated peers (Rendón, García, & Person, 2004). This social capital includes a knowledge base of college-going processes and procedures and the skill set to navigate them when questions arise. Often parents of marginalized students feel inferior about the college experience and do not get involved in academics, leaving their children to not only build their support networks on their own but also play the double role of student and teacher for their parents.

Identity Consciousness: Parent and Family Engagement and Outreach

Donovan and McKelfresh (2008) state,

> Rather than waiting until students arrive at the gates of higher education, colleges and universities must reach out to precollegiate students and their families, inviting them to campus events and programs to familiarize them with the campus community. Efforts to include first-generation students

and their families help them to avoid feeling like awkward "tourists" (Rodriguez, 2001, p. 146) on campus, uncomfortable with their surroundings, eager to go home to familiarity and comfort. (p. 396)

Providing the families of first-generation college students with opportunities to build social capital and become engaged with campus in an identity-conscious manner will help students feel supported in all aspects of their life, thereby contributing to their overall college success. This is particularly important because a profile of the experiences of first-generation college students and their families, generated by the Higher Education Research Institute in conjunction with the Cooperative Institutional Research Program, found that this group of students tends to be more reliant on their families (Saenz, Hurtado, Barrera, Wolf, & Yeung, 2007). These students are also more likely to want to live at home, which further necessitates involving their families in the campus community.

In addition to understanding the needs of first-generation college students and their families, student affairs professionals must also create programs that take into account the racial and ethnic backgrounds of their participants. As we prepare identity-conscious programming for this population, we must first be aware of the needs of the population we hope to serve and then create the programming to achieve those desired outcomes. We want first-generation families to be prepared for their student's transition to college. We know that these families, as a group, may not have the capital to understand what happens during orientation or the importance of that event, the academic rigor their student might face, or the large role they can play in their student's confidence to succeed. As these are the areas we hope to address, all the programs developed for this group should have learning outcomes that reflect these goals.

The majority of first-generation college students have historically come from Hispanic and African American ethnic and racial backgrounds, with Hispanic students representing the largest number of first-generation college students (Saenz et al., 2007). Cultural implications, such as expectations to live at home and contribute to the household, can be part of the conversation with families about ways to support their student's academic success. The college-going experience does not implicitly result in a detachment from the family unit. Again, knowing our target population allows us to develop strategies for success and design programs that address these concerns head-on.

Parental encouragement to attend and do well in college is important for first-generation students who often report that their parents are the reason they attend college. Sending the message that a college education can be a tool for upward mobility for the student, and therefore the family overall, can have a number of positive effects. These structured programs can increase students' capacity for building skills related to academic success (e.g., studying, writing, and overcoming barriers) while also increasing families' capacity to coach their students through processes such as gathering information and seeking support resources relevant to their needs. The fact that identity is not centered makes these types of programs unique. Student success is at the center, but the identities, and therefore potential systemic barriers, are acknowledged and understood so that a success plan can be implemented through programming.

Knowing that structured interventions for the families of first-generation college students and students of color can strengthen their support networks and increase student success is only one part of the equation. Having a plan in place for finding this at-risk population and enriching their experiences through programmatic efforts is the other part. The rest of this chapter describes how to create a comprehensive, identity-conscious parent and family engagement program.

Working With First-Generation Families and Families of Color

Once you have a firm understanding of who needs assistance through intervention, best practices for that intervention, and the specific needs of your target population, you can design programs that take into account all these areas. Interventions and programmatic efforts are most successful when you have a game plan that addresses the population you want to serve and what each programmatic offering will provide. Having this outline will allow you to allot the necessary resources and involve the necessary campus partners to make your program a success.

Finding Your Target Population

Identity-conscious programming requires you to clearly identify and understand the population you want to reach with your programs. This will guide everything you do, from outreach to this group to creating relationships with campus partners who will support the work being done. Clearly stating with whom you want to work and why members of this group need special attention will allow you to develop precise outcomes for your identity-conscious parent and family outreach programs.

When determining your target population, it is important to take your sphere of influence and locus of control into consideration. Where can you have the largest impact given the resources available to you? In the urban environment of my institution, outreach is targeted toward the families of first-generation students and students of color in the metro and suburban areas closest to the university. The families of first-generation college students who live at home and commute to campus can be immediately helped by outreach based on their geographic location.

To access demographic and contact information for this group, it is important to establish strong relationships with the campus partners who collect and distribute these data. Building a relationship with the office of admissions is the first step in developing a comprehensive program and will provide you with rich data on demographics, including racial and ethnic identity and first-generation status. The office of admissions will also provide the necessary contact information for your targeted group. Because this partnership is so important, it should be developed early and with an understanding of the needs of both your office and the office of admissions.

When developing this partnership, ask the office of admissions staff to include information about your program in their communications sent to the families of first-generation college students and students of color so the admissions staff will know about the services offered to families, determine which admissions counselors can promote your programs in the recruitment process, and set realistic expectations for the amount of communication sent to prospective and newly admitted students. With our partners in admissions, we set up a calendar for the regular stream of communication sent to admitted students, and then we worked together to determine how to incorporate our information into the normal admissions communication cycle so that it does not create an overwhelming workload for our partners.

Once a partnership is established with the office of admissions, the second step is designing a comprehensive program. A successful program will have a tiered outreach plan that involves parents and families in activities on and off campus. Events should concentrate on the families of first-year students and be scheduled before and at the end of the university orientation experience for a larger impact. For example, offer breakout sessions before orientation starts or after it concludes to involve your target families in the transformative curriculum you have developed. Maintaining communication and capacity building for these families can continue throughout the academic year with mailings, e-newsletters, and an on-campus event such as a weekend for families.

Introducing Your Program Early: The Preorientation Event

Prior to the university orientation, it is important to host an event for the families of first-generation college students and students of color to provide them with the opportunity to start creating a support network, gain knowledge about the orientation process, and meet the professionals who provide resources for student success. Offices that should participate in this program include the admissions office, to assist in connecting the recruitment process to the college transition process, and the financial aid office, to provide information on tuition and aid. In addition, representatives from the academic advising office can discuss the role advisers play in students' academic success and inform family members about your institution's academic rigor and its resources for help.

For the preorientation event to be successful, a representative from the office that runs the orientation should attend. Families of first-generation college students can find the orientation process overwhelming because a large amount of information is shared in a very short period of time. Students may be separated from their families throughout the day, and if the family of the student does not speak English and the institution only offers sessions in English, the language barrier will block them from having their questions answered. A campus partner who can share an overview of the full orientation experience, walk the families through the purpose of various orientation activities, and explain when and why students are separated from their families during orientation can relieve a lot of the anxiety tied to the orientation.

As the coordinator of this preorientation event, you need to ask the partners to organize their presentations to answer common questions they get during orientation and once students arrive on campus. While it might seem that you are simply repeating information that will be addressed at the upcoming orientation, targeted families often benefit from early exposure to crucial information, especially in a safe setting where they can ask more questions. Having preliminary stakeholder meetings in which goals are set and information is shared about the purpose of identity-conscious programs for families of first-generation college students and students of color ensures that everyone is receiving the same message.

Conclude the event with an overview of major points along with handouts that include contact information for the campus partners who participated. If you have a large base of non-English-speaking families in your target population, consider offering handouts in these families' native languages. Your overview should recap the financial, academic, and organizational resources that are available to the families. Families can leave the event with knowledge in hand and the reassurance that help is available if they need more guidance or support. Again, this event is about building the knowledge base for first-generation families so that their confidence going into orientation, and therefore their ability to truly participate in the sessions, is increased.

At the completion of our 2013 preorientation event, one parent of a student completed a survey and shared her thoughts on the benefits of attending this session together with her child:

> I learned about supporting and encouraging my student. I learned about managing my student's financing options, and I learned how essential it is to be involved. . . . As a parent, I appreciate the orientation for me to understand the challenges my child is going to face in difficult aspects, and the resources in helping my children in the transition.

This parent saw the value in serving as a partner on the student's academic journey, which the student also appreciated. In the same evaluation from 2013, the parent's student said,

> I learned that there is an immense amount of support at DePaul and I learned that there are many resources for guidance, but I also need my family to understand that I need to be on campus to use these services. I can't do it without their help, though.

Once this preorientation event concludes, first-generation college students and their families will be significantly more prepared to attend the regular university orientation program and reap the maximum benefit from the experience. The preorientation event establishes an understanding of college processes and procedures in a way that is less intimidating for first-generation families; it also allows them to have a better understanding of their important role in the student's success. When the resources that offices provide to students are framed around the specific needs of historically underrepresented groups, the impact is twofold. First, these identity-conscious efforts build capacity in families, which will pay dividends in students' success in college. Second, marginalized identities are explicitly named and celebrated in these events, serving as a form of empowerment and support for members of these communities as they enter higher education.

Keeping Momentum After Orientation: Hosting a Kickoff Event Before School Starts

Having an event for your target population before the academic year starts provides an opportunity to revisit some of what was introduced at the preorientation event and orientation, while also deepening your students' exposure to your curriculum for first-year success. The goal of the kickoff event should be to reinforce your institution's support for these families while also continuing to empower them to better communicate with and support their college-going children. This event can also be used to facilitate networking among families to develop peer support networks at the parent level as well as initiate or continue conversations between students and their families regarding expectations and values as the student makes the transition into college.

Having conversations about what the student's transition to college means for the family as a whole is invaluable. Interactive dialogue sessions on setting and clarifying expectations focuses the academic year on support rather than questions of financial assistance and expectations on communication, working, child care, or household chores. These conversations allow families to start the academic year without questions about how the student will be supported. Instead, the focus can be on capacity building for all parties that are concerned with the success of the student.

A kickoff event before the orientation should take place two to three weeks before students start their course work. It provides an additional opportunity for families to visit campus and see the spaces where their students will be learning, alleviating some of the concern they may have for this new journey. A sample agenda for an event such as this one is outlined in Figure 1.1.

This is just one example of an interactive event that provides social and skill-based support for your new first-generation college students, students of color, and their families. Scheduling events before and after orientation alleviates some of the nervousness in the college transition process while introducing key support services and resources. Maintaining the relationships fostered at these events throughout the academic year is the next step in creating a cohesive, identity-conscious parent and family program.

Maintaining Engagement Throughout the First Year

While providing on-campus opportunities to involve parents and families is important, it is not always financially or logistically feasible. A great way to maintain engagement with families and help them build knowledge is through a newsletter published a few times during the academic year. As first-generation college students are more likely to commute to campus from their homes, mailing addresses obtained from your office of admissions are a great way to send out literature to parents and families. Pairing this with electronic distribution of information has been an increasingly popular tool as it cuts down on costs considerably.

An ideal form of ongoing family engagement is a printed quarterly newsletter that provides pertinent information for families in a relevant, identity-conscious format. However, printing and mailing a hard copy of a newsletter is not always financially viable. One key way to keep costs low while providing this information is to place a quarterly newsletter on your departmental website, preferentially on a dedicated parent and family portal. Providing

Figure 1.1 Parent and family kickoff BBQ agenda.

Goal: To build a community of support while creating networking connections and building capital for parents and families of our students

Check-In

- One staff member to handle registration and hand out parking vouchers
- Music playing in the background
- Other staff members mingling
- Parents and families can grab breakfast items, mingle, and be seated
- PowerPoint will be activated with questions for mingling/introductions

Welcome

- Overview of Parent & Family Outreach Office and its initiatives
- Staff introductions
- Welcome (outlines purpose of the day)

Program-Facilitated Activity: Continuum

- Students will begin the activity by placing themselves onstage
- Staff member will read a college transition statement, and students will move along a continuum line: strongly agree (far left), neutral (middle), strongly disagree (far right)

  o I plan on calling my family every day
  o I plan on texting/e-mailing my family every day
  o I am nervous about moving from high school to college-level course work
  o I have a four-year plan for paying for college
  o I don't want to work so that I can focus on my studies
  o I plan on getting involved in at least one extracurricular activity

- Parents will continue the activity by placing themselves onstage
- Staff member will read a college transition statement, and parents will move along the continuum line: strongly agree (far left), neutral (middle), strongly disagree (far right)

  o My student should call/text/e-mail me every day
  o I am worried my student will get too engrossed in the social life at college
  o I am excited about all the new people my student will meet
  o My student and I have discussed what our family financial contribution can be for his or her college education
  o I expect my student to work more than 20 hours per week
  o I expect my student to help out at home (regularly, chores, babysitting, etc.)

- Parents, families, and students will gather together at a table to discuss the activity with guided questions such as:

  o (Parents to students) What surprised you about our expectations for each other?
  o (Students to parents) What surprised you about our expectations for each other?
  o Students, what can you do to help your parents eliminate any fears they might be having?
  o Parents, what can you do to help your students succeed?
  o Building a College Transition Success Plan (based on the previous activity and discussion)

Networking

- Parents and family members will be able to fill out the Networking Sheet provided to them at the beginning of check-in. This portion gives parents and families a chance to build their own network of support and resources, similar to what is asked of new students in the first weeks of an academic year.

Wrap-Up

- Let families know about the impact parent involvement has on student success
- List of events for parents, families, and students for the year
- End event with questions and answers

this digital content will steer families to your website while allowing easy access to the people and offices mentioned in your content. It is important, however, to recognize that computer or Internet access may not always be available in the homes of your target populations. A mailed postcard containing highlights of your digital content is a useful supplementary tool.

Your postcard should focus on a number of things. First, it should include the name and contact information of the professional staff coordinator of your family outreach program. Second, it should recap the newsletter's contents so that families who do not have Internet acces can follow up by telephone with the contact person about specific information. Third, providing the Web address for the digital newsletter will allow family members to access your document when they can.

The newsletters, whether hard copy or digital, should be thematically organized on issues students are facing, opportunities for students on campus and why they should take advantage of them, and topics that require familial involvement. Newsletters that empower families of first-generation students and students of color can be organized as follows:

Fall

- A welcome address from the parent and family outreach and empowerment coordinator
- An introduction to the college transition team
- Important dates and information related to a weekend planned for families

Winter

- Student involvement highlights and a testimonial from a student
- Tips to keep students on the path to degree completion
- Financial aid processes

Spring

- How a family's relationship with a student may change after the first year of college
- Avoiding the sophomore slump
- What's next for the students in your department

The focus of the newsletter is to provide parents and families with pertinent information directly. The content areas, such as navigating financial aid or preparing for the student's sophomore transition, are particularly salient to first-generation families who might not have any knowledge about these things. The newsletter should be written in family-friendly language rather than in the technical language normative in higher education circles to enhance family members' ability to use the information. In addition to the detailed content provided in each newsletter, it is also important to remind the families that they are still a valued part of their children's education and are paramount in helping them to succeed. In today's budget landscape, holding large-scale events across the course of an academic year can be cost prohibitive. Front-loading these on-campus events has enormous benefits for building trust-based relationships with historically marginalized families, but we must also maintain some form of interaction throughout the first year. Newsletter content is easy to access and can be changed year to year to address key concerns for your targeted population as you continue to develop your identity-conscious family engagement program.

This newsletter series can act as a bridge throughout the academic year. Looking back, families of first-generation college students and students of color will see that from the moment their children were accepted at an institution, the families were provided with resources to help them understand their role in student success and strategies for maintaining that success throughout the first year. Throughout each engagement opportunity, families of first-generation college students and students of color should be given the message that they matter to your institution and to their children's success. Through in-person events and ongoing newsletters, you will send the message repeatedly that families' support, guidance, and awareness of issues facing their children will have an impact on students' success. Reiterating this message for families who have not always recognized their role in their children's college-going experience is the basis for a successful identity-conscious family engagement program.

Assessment: How Do You Know It Works?

To understand if learning outcomes of parent and family engagement programs were being met, we distributed and collected evaluations on each program offered. Attendees were asked to respond to questions on their understanding of resources, their comfort with critical conversations with their student, and their confidence in creating an action plan with their student regarding expectations of each other during the first year of college. Overall, participants reported that their understanding of resources in our particular office and across campus was enhanced as a result of participating in our events. Participants regularly reported that they came to see their relationship with their student as a partnership and that by having an understanding of procedures, family members were able to guide students to the places and people who would support them from the university's perspective. This was demonstrated by a decrease in the number of incidents where our first-generation college students reported not being supported by their families that attended these events. Based on the past few years of data collection for outreach programs, we look forward to continuing to provide an opportunity for parents and families to reinforce their orientation experience with information about the offices and resources available to them. However, we have come to understand the importance of playing a more targeted role during orientation, which came to fruition during the summer 2015 orientation cycle with a specialized breakout session for families of first-generation college students and students of color. This program highlighted the importance of family engagement in student success, empowering families by introducing them to literature and data on their contribution to university metrics on student success. Although we have used a digital newsletter series to provide pertinent information related to student success and family support during the academic year, we were not having much success tracking usage and interaction with families via this outlet. We have recently launched a blog for families that still disseminates this information but provides us with real-time data on traffic and the popularity of specific posts and allows us to tailor information based on need, such as adding information on processes, financial aid, or psychosocial support of students.

The collection of feedback regarding satisfaction and knowledge acquisition has allowed us to amend regularly offered programs each year to meet the changing needs of our students and their families. Being more engaged with families during orientation and introducing our blog early has already driven up traffic to the site and has allowed us to start offering our campus partners information about the impact of our programming earlier and more regularly. All these steps keep our comprehensive identity-conscious parent and family programming fresh and relevant for our program participants.

Conclusion

Families have a strong influence on their students' academic careers. Involving the families of first-generation college students and students of color and educating them about the college-going experience in general and major milestones and possible pitfalls in the first year in particular is our duty as professionals who support these students. Putting in the time and resources needed to facilitate these programs can pay huge dividends. If our student Doria, along with her family, had participated in the series of events provided to her and her family as a first-generation college student of color, they would have had the opportunity to hear from campus partners regarding academic rigor and support. She would have participated in activities that led her family through a discussion about expectations on working and dedicated study time. Although she undoubtedly would have met challenges in her first year of college, as is normal, she might have been able to turn to her family for support in mitigating these challenges.

The success of the identity-conscious parent and family engagement programs I have overseen is evident in the decreased number of students coming to my office afraid or unsure of how to tell their family a financial hold has been placed on their academic record or that they failed a test. Instead, I am hearing stories of students who are getting reminders not only from me but also from their families about the approaching deadline for the Free Application for Federal Student Aid or about our family weekend programming. I am hearing stories of students who can study at home because their families have worked with them to set study hours in lieu of chores. Most important, I am hearing stories of students who are being told they can succeed and who thrive because they are supported in their home and at their university.

Action Items

While a multifaceted curriculum to involve the families of first-generation college students and students of color is an endeavor that has a lot of moving parts, it allows them to reap benefits by reinforcing the tenets of student success for all stakeholders. The following action steps can help get a full curriculum off the ground.

1. Establish one person as a point of contact. Designating one person in your department or division to act as a point of contact enables you to establish trust and obtain acceptance from students' parents and other family members. Parents and family members of these college students are often overwhelmed by the number of offices they have to navigate to support their students. Offering a one-stop resource can empower them to more actively communicate with staff at your institution.

2. Understand your student and family constituents. Each university has its own unique student population and goals for enabling various target groups to succeed. A good understanding of this and the metrics of your programs can help justify costs associated with running an identity-conscious parent and family program and underscore the need for this type of programming for students' off-campus support systems. If your institution is particularly focused on four- or six-year graduation rates, track this metric as you assess the impact of your program, beginning with

an in-depth study of first- to second-year persistence rates for your targeted students. If your institution is more concerned about first-generation students and students of color leaving the institution, tracking the yearly retention and attrition patterns of your targeted students is critical.

3. Create on-campus events before and after orientation. Campus programs designed specifically for first-generation families will do the following: (a) provide family members with direct access to the office personnel they will hear from during orientation; (b) help families understand the kinds of questions they can and should be asking before the actual event; and (c) give first-generation families an opportunity to return to campus after orientation, create communities, and start to address expectations for mutual communication with their children. Your point person should be present at each event so that a content area expert will be available if families have questions about how to support, encourage, and be champions for their children.

4. Build strong relationships with campus partners. An understanding of the ways campus partners can have an impact on the experiences of students and their family members allows you to fill any gaps in meeting the needs of first-generation students and families through identity-conscious initiatives. Great working relationships with these partners make it easier to implement and gain support for your unique offerings. Students need the entire university network to make their experience successful, and a coalition to empower your targeted families will be more effective than you working alone.

References

Donovan, J. A., & McKelfresh, D. A. (2008). In community with students' parents and families. *NASPA Journal, 45*(3), 384–405.

Jacobson, J. (2003, July 18). Help not wanted. *Chronicle of Higher Education.* Retrieved from chronicle.com/article/Help-Not-Wanted/19620

Mathews, J. (2007, November 5). New study gives hovering college parents extra credit. *Washington Post.* Retrieved from www.washingtonpost.com

Rendón, L. I., García, M., & Person, D. (Eds.). (2004). *Transforming the first year of college for students of color* (Monograph No. 38). Columbia: University of South Carolina, National Resource Center for The First-Year Experience and Students in Transition.

Saenz, V. B., Hurtado, S., Barrera, D., Wolf, D., & Yeung, F. (2007). *First in my family: A profile of first-generation college students at four-year institutions since 1971.* Los Angeles: Higher Education Research Institute, University of California, Los Angeles.

2

RETAINING AND GRADUATING EMPOWERED MEN OF COLOR

Eric Mata and André Bobb

G rowing up, Michael split time between the south side of Chicago and the south suburbs, where he graduated from high school. He was the oldest of three children being raised by a single mother. He was from a working-class family, came from an underperforming high school, and commuted more than an hour to and from campus. Although he was a little skeptical about joining the Men of Color Initiative, he decided to give it a shot and became heavily involved in the program. Michael faced many trials throughout his college career, including losing his mother in his senior year. Considering all these factors, data show that Michael should have been less likely than his peers to persist through to graduation. But he graduated. He is working in a full-time job he enjoys while he continues to look after his younger brothers.

After graduation, Michael said he doesn't believe he would have made it through college if it were not for the structured support and opportunities the Men of Color Initiative provided for him. Through his roles as a participant and a staff member of the program, he came to understand who he was as a man—and, more important, he came to understand himself as a Black man and the importance that identity carried for him.

Overview

During the past decade, there has been a dearth of programs addressing the rock-bottom retention rates of male students of color on college campuses across the country. With six-year graduation rates at 35.1% for African

American men and 47.4% for Latino men (National Center for Education Statistics, 2015), a loud and reverberating voice called out to college campuses to do more to increase graduation rates for these students. A response to this call was the establishment of myriad programs designed to work solely with male students of color. Feeling as though more could be done, an initiative, backed by the White House, called My Brother's Keeper was established by President Barack Obama to "address persistent opportunity gaps faced by boys and young men of color and ensure that all young people can reach their full potential" ("My Brother's Keeper," 2014).

Although the focus on the retention of male students of color is important, one thing we believe has been lacking is the incorporation of empowerment into these men's programs. Although a community-building focus is important, particularly at historically White institutions, a focus on empowerment allows a deeper and more meaningful exploration of the intersectionality of identity that exists for our students. This focus allows us to move students from wanting to be around those with whom they share identities to a place where they understand how to navigate a world with people who may not always look like them.

This chapter outlines key research areas focused on curricular models for men of color programs and best practices being used across the country; provides an in-depth look into the Men of Color Initiative at a large, private, urban university and how we infused retention and empowerment into its creation; and presents tangible action items student affairs professionals can use in the development of empowerment-focused support programs for male students of color.

Chapter Framework

Men of color—outnumbered, underinvolved, and underengaged—are leaving our campuses in droves. According to Harper (2013), these trends have been a cause for alarm among college educators, administrators, and policymakers across the country and have often led to the development of programs that are rooted in deficit-based thinking and solely focused on how we can change or "fix" our men of color.

Harper (2014) suggests that we have been looking at the experiences of male students of color from the wrong perspective. The alarmist perspective that has dominated academic research as well as national media has focused primarily on shifting the blame for differential achievement onto men of color on our campuses. Through his research, Harper was able to determine that the majority of men of color programs focused on establishing mentoring programs, developing one- to two-day summits, and creating centers on college campuses designed to provide safe spaces for students in these programs. Even as recently as 2011 researchers Lee and Ransom released an extensive report outlining the lack of success males of color were experiencing in the educational landscape.

To move away from the deficit approach to addressing retention and graduation rates as well as underengagement among men of color, Harper (2013) suggests that the development of men of color programs should start with standards that move beyond the social and community-building aspects that are often at the core of engaging men. Additionally, program administrators should understand the intersection of race and gender and how this has an impact on the ways young men of color participate in and progress through our programs. The identity-conscious approach Harper suggests has been a cornerstone in our development of the Men of Color Initiative.

Identity Consciousness

A distinction needs to be made between identity-centered programs and identity-conscious programs. The development of men of color programs has primarily been driven by low matriculation and graduation rates across the country as 60% to 65% of men of color will not graduate from our colleges and universities. This focus is considered to be identity centered because a direct line is drawn from a student's identity as a man of color to low graduation rates. The underlying assumption is that because they are male and students of color, they will more than likely need to be involved in a men's program or they will probably not graduate.

An alternative program is developed with an identity-conscious lens. This approach seeks to examine the various identities and experiences commonly present in men of color. Furthermore, it seeks to analyze how the intersection of these various identities and experiences affect the ways students experience the university. This approach doesn't end with men of color as the identity-centered approach does; it begins with it, then digs deeper. An identity-conscious approach in the development of a men of color program considers the importance not only of graduation but also of creating opportunities for participants to engage in critical reflection on the ways their race and their socialization as men might affect, support, or impede their ability to be successful. Moreover, an identity-conscious approach forces us to consider that myriad factors connected to other identities might also have an impact on a student's ability to be successful. For example, in analyzing data at your institution, you might want to include variables such as Pell Grant eligibility, first-generation status, and geographic location to discern whether characteristics beyond race and gender might factor into a student's experience on your campus.

A question we found ourselves continually asking was this: What do we know to be true about our students? We found a lot of answers through qualitative and quantitative research. Similar to the trends in the key research, we knew that we had a relatively small population of students, we knew that four-year graduation rates were low, and we knew that our students were underengaged. This raised the question, What do we know to be true about how to address those realities?

For us, the answer was empowerment, which to us is about providing programs that give students permission to be successful. Building an empowerment program is about crafting interventions rooted in individual and systemic barriers to success while maintaining an identity-conscious approach. Although we believe everything a student needs to be successful can be found on our campus, we know that often our men of color are not using the services available to them for a number of reasons. Therefore, we set out to create a program that would address the barriers to involvement while empowering students to gain a better understanding of themselves as young men of color. For us, a measure of success for the participants in the Men of Color Initiative would not simply be increased persistence and graduation rates but also increased participation rates in the curricular and cocurricular experiences that drive student success.

Building the Men of Color Initiative

The Men of Color Initiative was developed to address low retention and graduation rates for male students of color with a particular focus on students from our region. A working group consisting of faculty, staff, and students was pulled together to research the state of male students of color across the country. Their charge was to create a series of recommendations that could be developed into a funding proposal, which led to the creation of the program.

Initially, the program was designed on two basic premises, the first being that incoming students need a peer guide to help them with the transition to campus. This was addressed through the development of a peer mentor component in the program. The second premise was the notion that male students of color need to feel a sense of community. This was addressed by creating intentional large-group social events that were focused on building community. We came to realize through anecdotal evidence and focus groups that to maintain students' interest in the program after the first year, we needed to create a multiyear, multitiered program that created unique experiences for them throughout their tenure at DePaul University.

These unique experiences were clustered as cohort experiences according to the students' year in school. A distinct outcome for each year is based on where students are on their university trajectory. For first-year students, the focus was on leadership development. The second year was focused on career discernment and the intersection of identity and career choice. The third year was focused on putting skills into action, and the final year was focused on preparing students for the transition to life after college.

Year 1: Men of Color Initiative Leadership Academy

Year 1 of the Men of Color Initiative focuses on preparing our first-year men of color by providing them with the tools necessary to succeed in their first year of college. Although a number of different factors contribute to the success of our students during their first year, we believe emphasis on the following are the most important: (a) building academic success skills, (b) using university resources, and (c) developing a healthy social network. These three themes are covered in the Men of Color Initiative Leadership Academy, a biweekly seminar-style series of workshops, presentations, and conversations that allow students to explore what it takes to achieve academic success. An underlying theme that cut across all three factors was a continuous conversation about the role students' identities as men of color played in their experiences on campus.

Building academic skills. Students come to the university with various levels of academic preparation. We know that the higher a students' high school quality index, the more likely they are to have received adequate academic preparation for the collegiate level. Additionally, if their parents or relatives attended college before them, students are more likely to be aware of the tools needed—beyond content knowledge in a particular subject—to attain academic success. What we also know is that our students come from a wide range of high schools, and they may or may not be first-generation college students. Because of this, it was important to develop a first-year curriculum that made no assumptions about our participants' level of academic preparation.

We believe students should have certain skills, regardless of their preparedness level, to ensure their academic success. These skills include study habits, time management, goal setting, navigating academic resources, and help-seeking behaviors. During the first academic quartner, the Leadership

Academy implemented the following workshop sessions to help students develop their skills:

- Study Tips Testimonials: Story Sharing by Upperclassmen
- Where Did All My Time Go? Tips on Effective Self (Time) Management
- Setting S.M.A.R.T. Academic Goals
- Going Beyond Google: Navigating the University Library Database
- I Think I Need Help in This Class: What Do I Do?

These workshops help students to not only build academic skills but also become familiar with university resources.

Using university resources. Most of our students commute to campus on a daily basis, with a large portion of them coming from several neighborhoods away. Many of these students also have off-campus jobs and other responsibilities that limit the amount of time they are able to spend on campus. Even in the face of these realities, we know that students who use the university's resources and are more involved on campus are more likely to be retained. Therefore, we find it imperative for all our students to be aware of and connected to the various resources our university provides.

We asked ourselves the following questions:

- Are our students aware of university-sponsored Study Jams, where free math and writing tutors are available?
- Are they familiar with our university's employment website and the number of employers throughout the region who want to hire our students?
- Have they visited our career services office to have their résumé reviewed?
- Have they attended a presentation delivered by our financial fitness staff to begin learning about credit cards and whether one is right for them?
- Do they know the dates for student involvement fairs or the process for finding and joining a student organization?
- Do they know where the financial aid office is located, and do they know that the best time to speak to someone from that office is before they realize there is a hold on their student account?

These questions, and many more like them, are at the forefront of what we call the Utilizing the University Resources curriculum. Our goal is to identify the university resources that are most essential to a student's success in the first year and ensure that our participants are aware of the fact that these resources exist. The truth of the matter, however, is that awareness alone is not enough.

Although our participants may be able to identify the resources that are available to them, this does not ensure that they will take the necessary next step in using these services. One key factor that increases the probability that a student will use the services of a particular office or department is whether the student knows at least one person who works there. We have found that if our participants are able to be acquainted with at least one person in an office or department, they are more likely to take advantage of the services the office provides. Because of this, we make concerted efforts to bring in guest speakers from across campus so they can make a personal connection with our Men of Color Initiative participants, thereby increasing the probability that our students will make use of that office.

An example of this involves a key partnership with the university's library. By organizing a library usage session, we were able to debunk the myth that libraries are merely a quiet place to study. Our students learned about various tools and services the library provides, such as access to library databases, individualized research assistance, a statewide library book-sharing program, and our library's Ask a Librarian instant messaging service, among others. Perhaps more important, Men of Color Initiative participants also made a personal connection with a full-time librarian willing to assist them in using each of these services. The session's participants acknowledged that they had rarely, if ever, been to the library prior to visiting it as participants with the Men of Color Initiative but that after the session they would be more likely to visit it. This session was pivotal in moving toward *increasing* awareness about the library while simultaneously *decreasing* the social stigma that often prevents men of color from using the library's services. It also enabled Men of Color Initiative participants to make a connection with a university staff member who could become part of their social network.

Developing a healthy social network. College is one of the most transformative developmental periods in a young person's life; therefore, it is essential for students to be surrounded by positive social support systems that are important for a positive developmental process. One key question that is central to our theme of developing a healthy social network is, How do the people around a student add value? To adequately answer this question, Men of Color Initiative participants are asked to think about their own personal values and where these values come from. They are also asked to think about their short-term and long-term goals socially, academically, and spiritually and to think about the company they keep and to assess whether these individuals add value to their life based on their stated values and goals. Men of

Color Initiative participants are encouraged to expand their social networks, either through joining student organizations, being a part of an academic study group, or having friends who help them take their mind off school work for short periods of time. The point is to get our participants to a place where they are able to determine what a healthy social network looks like for them, then help them begin to actually develop that network. Men of Color Initiative participants use this network, as well as the skills and resources they have developed in their first year, as a foundation for making identity-conscious decisions about their future career path.

Year 2: Career Academy

In the second year of the program, students are invited to participate in the Men of Color Initiative Career Academy. The target population of this component is students in their sophomore year or first-year transfer students to the university. Similar to a leadership academy, our Career Academy is a seminar-style program, but it is focused on providing students with experiences that allow them to take part in career discernment experiences. Throughout the year, students are invited to critically reflect on the following questions: Who am I? Who can I become? How do I get there? Throughout the year, each of these questions is examined through the lenses of race and gender.

Who am I? As an entry into the Who am I? portion of the Career Academy curriculum, participants are invited to explore their social identities using a variation on the basic identity mapping exercise. In our exercise students are given a worksheet and asked to write down their social identities under eight social identity markers (race/ethnicity, gender, sexual orientation, ability/disability, religion/religious affiliation, socioeconomic class, size/appearance, and other) inside designated circles around the perimeter of the worksheet. The worksheet also has a space in the center for the students to write their name. Once students have completed the worksheet, they are then asked to share the messages they received as boys and young men about what it means to be successful. This brainstorming session allows us to explore the ways in which the participants' various identity markers, such as race or class, interact with their masculinity and often result in the young men feeling pressured to pursue degrees that are centered on making money as a mark of success.

It is no surprise that a healthy majority of the young men of color who come into the program are clustered in business, science, and law-related majors. The end goal of this particular set of curricular exercises is to encourage students to challenge their thinking on what they define as *successful*. Ideally, students begin to understand what their passions and values are in a way that encourages the exploration of new career fields more aligned with who they come to understand themselves to be as young men of color.

Who can I become? Once a student has either solidified a decision about his intended major or has begun to explore new career options, it is important for participants to be able to clearly articulate whom they want to become when they graduate. One of the things Eric noticed once we began to explore career discernment efforts in the Men of Color Initiative was that students who were confident in their major and career path could not readily describe their postcollege career plans in detail. For example, when Eric asked an accounting student what he wanted to do after he graduated, he said, "I want to be an accountant."

It is obvious that an accounting major would want to become an accountant, so Eric pressed the student for more information. Where do you want to be an accountant? Which one of the Big Four accounting firms? Why that one? Have you explored internship opportunities? Most of the students were not able to answer any of these questions with any amount of certainty. These types of questions are particularly challenging for students with no direct line connecting a major to a specific career. The main goal of this portion of the second-year curriculum is to encourage students to explore the possibilities in their intended major. We have found that students who take career tests on websites such as Sokanu understand not only what they might do in a specific career but also understand career trajectories and salary expectations.

How do I get there? The remainder of the second year for program participants is focused on developing a plan to meet their intended career or graduate program goals by the time they graduate. Students are encouraged to develop a detailed timeline for obtaining the relevant experiences they will need to be successful. For most students this involves, but is not limited to, seeking and obtaining an internship, engaging in informational meetings with people in their intended career, participating in career center programs, and developing relationships with faculty members in their chosen disciplines.

Year 3: Faculty Mentoring

The Faculty Mentoring component is a newer addition to the program. As program participants emerge from the Career Academy with a focus on taking steps to ensure career or graduate school success, it is important to provide them with continued support in their endeavors. Studies have shown that students who develop active relationships with faculty members in their discipline are much more engaged in the classroom. Harper (2012) states that "working closely on educationally purposeful tasks outside the classroom afforded the [faculty] and [students] substantive opportunities to learn about each other, which added value to the students' achievement trajectories in myriad ways" (p. 18). Placing the Faculty Mentoring program in a student's junior year was intentional for three reasons. First, at that time, students are moving more heavily into major courses, and we felt it was important to have a faculty mentor who could provide insight into course selection. Second, we wanted to provide an opportunity for students to develop relationships with faculty members who were expressly interested in their success as male students of color. Third, we wanted students to develop and build on their networking and relationship-building skills in a predetermined setting.

A popular assumption in the field of student affairs is that it is difficult to develop relationships with faculty on our campuses. We found the opposite to be true when soliciting faculty members to participate in the program. The key for us was to establish a working relationship with someone on our university's faculty council (a version of an academic senate), who could then be our point person for disseminating information across the different schools and colleges. The faculty council member who was our point person issued a call for mentors, and we were able to draw a lot of interest in the program.

A challenge we faced was finding a way to turn faculty interest in mentoring into a commitment. Through some conversations with campus partners, we found the best way to move from interest to commitment was by making the process of signing up to be a mentor as simple as possible. The first step was sending out the call for interested faculty, which netted more than 30 faculty members from almost every college and school. From there we were able to obtain a more meaningful commitment by contacting interested faculty and asking them to respond to three questions related to their time commitments, their desire to participate, and what they wanted to get out of the program. Through this step, we were able to recruit 15 faculty members who were committed to working with the program participants. Inviting interested faculty to submit a response to two or three basic questions allowed them to move from being an interested to a committed faculty mentor.

Year 4: Senior Transitions

As program participants get closer to graduation, it is important to prepare them for long-term success. The Senior Transitions component of the Men of Color Initiative is designed to do just that. By engaging students in a series of workshops designed to explore the intersection of success and their identities as men of color and the tangible steps needed to graduate, they are able to explore how they as men can have an impact on or impede their ability to be successful. A key component of the Senior Transitions program involves giving students career-related experiences that can have a positive impact on their success in life after college.

Throughout the senior year, students are asked to meet with Men of Color Initiative staff to develop and implement a tangible plan that would lead to that success. For example, a year-long plan would include the following: participation in a personal values exercise, résumé and cover letter review with career center staff, participation in a campuswide job or graduate school fair, informational interview with Men of Color Initiative alumni in the desired field, mock interviews using the InterviewStream website, and budgeting for life postcollege. This and the other complex components of the Men of Color Initiative are successful because we intentionally develop a strong team of student staff to support our efforts.

Student Staff Development

The Men of Color Initiative holds weekly staff meetings to discuss relevant issues and outreach efforts and to plan large-group experiences. A couple of years into the start of the program, we added a section to the meeting agenda called Eric's Reflection. By introducing this reflection into staff meetings, we were able to explore the intersection of race and masculinity (as well as other identities) in ways that were tangible and authentic. This section was last on the agenda, and the premise behind it was twofold: First, it would be an opportunity to talk about current events or topics relevant to our student leaders in the Men of Color Initiative's experiences as men of color in America. Second, Eric modeled a form of vulnerability in his reflections that the student leaders found extremely engaging and compelling. Rather than share research and new academic findings in this closing reflection, Eric centered his short talks on his personal life, family challenges, and spiritual journey, as these dimensions connected with various elements of public life and the issues of importance to the student leaders.

Some of the topics we have covered ranged from the death of Trayvon Martin to the fear of raising a boy of color safely in the United States. These reflections were unscripted and based on what was happening in our own personal lives. We found it fascinating how the introduction of this reflection changed the dynamic of the meetings, which went from being really brief encounters to lasting two hours. We often had to cut the conversation short because we had reached the end of our scheduled time. These conversations were the fodder for planning our large-group experiences for the program.

Large-Group Experiences

Throughout the continued development of the Men of Color Initiative, it became increasingly important to distinguish the needs of program participants at multiple junctures of their college career. By creating unique experiences for students based on where they were in their career trajectory, we were able to create a multiyear, multipronged approach to addressing the myriad issues they face throughout their college experience. However, we also realized that large-scale programs that engaged the larger community in issues relevant to our target population were needed.

All Men of Color Initiative participants are encouraged to join our large-group community-building outings. These social events include attending a sporting event, going to a restaurant for pizza, or friendly competition at the bowling alley. Although no direct learning outcomes are associated with these outings, the goals are for our participants to experience positive male interactions, build camaraderie with other men of color on campus, and develop an affinity for the Men of Color Initiative.

Through our Men's Forums, we were able to tackle a range of issues through structured dialogic experiences. While each stage of the Men of Color Initiative experience (from Leadership Academy to Senior Transitions) has an underlying theme that focuses on the role of participants' identities as men of color and their collegiate and career experiences, with the Men's Forums, themes are not so subtle. These open discussions, which take place at least once per quarter, are focused primarily on the intersections of race and masculinity (among other identities) and the ways these identities dictate how we are viewed in the media; the impact they might have on our acceptance of the lesbian, gay, bisexual, transgender, and questioning community; how they construct our views and behaviors regarding sex; how they affect the ways society chooses to deal with us; and more. These forums are open to the public to encourage a diversity of thought, which tends to stimulate deep and enriching conversations.

The large-group experiences help create community among program participants as well as affinity for the program itself that contributes to a student's willingness to participate in our academy. The student leaders in the program played an integral part in the planning of large-group and community-building experiences. For us, the student leader experiences helped to serve as a bridge between the administrative and programmatic components of the program and the students' day-to-day experiences.

Assessment: How Do You Know It Works?

Early in the program we knew it would be important to assess program participation in relation to students who chose not to be involved. It was important for us to maintain accurate records to ensure that our data and metrics were accurate. To do this we created an Access database to track student information (including name, contact, and demographic information), quarterly grade point average (GPA), and credit hours attempted and earned. For the program, *success* is defined as meeting Satisfactory Academic Progress (SAP), which means obtaining at least a 2.5 GPA and earning 48 credit hours (a full load in the quarter system) for the academic year. Achieving SAP is directly correlated with a student's ability to graduate in four years.

Collecting this type of data allowed us to run success metrics in house, and we were able to determine that program participants were more likely to begin their second year as sophomores than their peers were. Additionally, after looking at two cohorts' worth of graduation data, we were able to see that program participants were more likely to graduate in four years than their peers. Initially, our focus was on looking strictly at first- to second-year retention data. We found this type of data collection to be a sort of false positive in that it was telling us that our students were coming back at higher rates than every other college population, but it was not translating to four-, five- and six-year graduation rates. This realization made us look more closely at academic progress data to determine the interventions and learning outcomes we needed to develop for the program.

The next level of assessment we are adding to the program is focused on understanding the types of learning students are experiencing as a result of their participation in the program. Combined with the impact assessment, this will allow us to better determine the ways the Men of Color Initiative is affecting the experiences of students in the program in relation to those who chose not to be involved. We believe this tiered assessment will be important to incorporate when developing a campus program for male students of color.

Conclusion

Michael came into his own throughout the four years he was enrolled in the program. He entered the university as a soft-spoken young man of color and left as a vibrant Black man who was committed to supporting other young men of color. He went from being a program participant in his first year to serving as a paid student mentor for the rest of his time at the university because he wanted to provide the same experience he had to other students. Through his experiences in the program, Michael was able to engage in deep and meaningful conversations about what it meant to be a man of color, and more specifically, a Black man on campus and in the larger context of this country.

Those of us who work with first-generation students and students of color know that social identity matters. We know that our social identities have an impact on the ways we experience the world. Our staff has begun to think about the difference between identity-centered and identity-conscious men of color programs. Each type of program calls us to engage with our students differently. The former tells us that men of color matter to us because they are men of color. It tells us that we should develop a program for men of color simply because they are not reaching the level of success that other students on our campuses are reaching. The latter tells us that men of color experience the world through the intersection of race and masculinity, and therefore interventions need to be created using a lens with this particular focus. A program rooted in being identity conscious ultimately creates opportunities for participants to understand the ways race and gender influence and affect their ability to be successful in college. It also tells us that the interventions and opportunities we create to reach the levels of success that keep them on par with their peers will need to be intentional to address the ways their identities matter.

Action Items

We have strived to build a multiyear, multitiered empowerment program for the participants of the Men of Color Initiative. Through a series of iterations, we feel as though we have a solid foundation on which to continue to build. As word has gotten out about the work we are doing, we have been contacted regularly to talk about our program. Eric often provided the following action items for individuals interested in developing a men of color support and advocacy program on their campuses.

1. Explore the needs of students on your campus. Multitiered experiences and large-group communal experiences are key to the long-term success of the program. We encourage you to determine the needs of the students on your campus based on their year on campus. Ask yourself: What do our first-year students struggle with? What do our sophomore students need from a men of color program? What do all of our students need throughout their experience in the university?

2. Identify and specifically target students who are struggling. It would have been easy for us to create a program that was open to all men of color at our institution; however, it was important for us to be able to disaggregate our data to find out which individuals in our target population were struggling and to make a concerted effort to reach out to them in particular. Ask yourself: Are all men of color struggling? Are there intersections we can use to mine our data to determine who needs the program the most?

3. Take an identity-conscious approach. As stated earlier, a certain amount of intentionality is important when working with young men of color who sit at the intersection of race and masculinity. Ask yourself: What is the impetus for this program? Do I want to create a safe space for our men of color to experience cultural enrichment, or do I want to create a safe space where our men of color can be challenged to explore the ways their identities have an impact on their experiences on our campus that result in increased persistence and timely graduation?

4. Make use of institutional data. We found that exploring success metrics and persistence rates are better indicators of student success. Essentially, this means that if students begin their second year on campus with enough credits to be officially considered sophomores and they have a GPA above 2.5, we know they are on the path toward graduation. And as students continue to meet these standards, we know they are persisting toward the ultimate goal of higher education: degree completion. Access to these data is only made possible by a partnership with our institutional research office. Ask yourself: What institutional partnership can I take advantage of to obtain the type of data necessary to make intentional, informed decisions related to our target population? How can I use institutional data to increase investment in my Men of Color Initiative from key institutional leaders?

References

Harper, S. R. (2012). *Black male student success in higher education: A report from the national Black male college achievement study.* Philadelphia: University of Pennsylvania, Center for the Study of Race and Equity in Education.

Harper, S. R. (2013). *Five things student affairs administrators can do to improve success among college men of color.* Retrieved from www.naspa.org/images/uploads/main/5THINGS-MOC.pdf

Harper, S. R. (2014). (Re)setting the agenda for college men of color: Lessons learned from a 15-year movement to improve Black male student success. In R.A. Williams (Ed.), *Men of color in higher education: New foundations for developing models for success* (pp. 116–143). Sterling, VA: Stylus.

Lee, J. M., & Ransom, T. (2011). *The educational experience of young men of color: A review of research, pathways, and progress.* Retrieved from youngmenofcolor.col legeboard.org/sites/default/files/downloads/EEYMC-ResearchReport.pdf

My brother's keeper. (2014). Retrieved from www.whitehouse.gov/my-brothers-keeper

National Center for Education Statistics. (2015). *Graduation rate from first institution attended for first-time, full-time bachelor's degree-seeking students at 4-year post-secondary institutions, by race/ethnicity, time to completion, sex, control of institution, and acceptance rate: Selected cohort entry years, 1996 through 2007.* Retrieved from http://nces.ed.gov/programs/digest/d14/tables/dt14_326.10.asp

3

IDENTITY-CONSCIOUS APPROACHES TO FIRST-YEAR, PEER-TO-PEER RETENTION PROGRAMS

Sara Furr

Becky followed the critical incident protocol perfectly. She submitted an online incident report and sent a text message to Larry, the program graduate assistant, alerting him to the report. I came into the office the next day and had a copy of the report in my inbox to review. Becky had met with her mentee, Matthew, for the second time. Matthew said he had not taken his anxiety medication since arriving on campus. He was having trouble sleeping, focusing in class, and feeling like himself. He told Becky he couldn't afford the medication. He was from out of state and living in a residence hall. His mom was a single parent, and he had younger siblings. He told Becky he was receiving just enough financial aid, scholarships, and grants to cover the cost of tuition and room and board. He didn't think he was going to last the quarter, let alone four years. Becky was spot on to be concerned about this. She informed Matthew that she would give this information to her supervisors, and someone from the office would contact him.

After calling Becky to clarify a few points in her report, I called Matthew to schedule a meeting, and he came in that afternoon. I asked how he was adjusting to the city and campus. I let him know that I had spoken with Becky and had the information she provided, but I wanted to hear his story in his own words. He talked about his financial distress and fear about continuing at the university. He knew his aid covered his basic needs but didn't know how he could afford his medication. After hearing Matthew's story, I asked if he would be willing to share his financial aid information with me.

He logged on to my computer and pulled up his financial aid information, and we printed out a copy to work from.

After reviewing his aid, I knew Matthew would be getting a small refund check. I talked with Matthew about his other needs: books, any additional medication, whether he had a meal plan to cover all his meals. I asked him about other financial support he might have from his family or a job. He did not have a job but was looking, and although he didn't have a relationship with his father, he had agreed to pay for books. After assuring Matthew that his package would cover all his costs to the university and get him a small refund, we talked budget. He had never managed a personal budget before and was nervous about getting what felt like a large sum of money all at once. I gave him the refund distribution schedule, and we talked about several ways to manage his money each quarter, especially making sure his funds would last from one quarter to the next. We also talked about ways to ensure that he would maintain his scholarships and grants. Later that year, Matthew returned to our office to talk about moving off campus. He thought he could save money that way but wasn't sure. We talked about all the projected expenses, ways to save with roommates, and so on.

Matthew thrived his freshman year. The following year he became a mentor and spent the next three years mentoring first-year students who were just like him.

Overview

The first- to second-year transition has long been touted as one of the most important areas of focus for retention and persistence efforts. Peer-to-peer mentoring became increasingly popular in higher education in the early 1990s. This formal mentoring process is widely believed to be related to positive outcomes for the mentor and the mentee (Ragins & Cotton, 1999; Seibert, 1999). Reasons for mentoring include institutional goals such as recruitment and retention of students (Jacobi, 1991) and pedagogical goals such as increasing learning and enhancing relationships with faculty and other students (Upcraft & Gardner, 1989). In the competition for recruitment and retention of students, colleges and universities offer a myriad of programs, support services, and resources. In a 1991 literature review, Jacobi concluded that "the concept of mentoring remains unclear and imprecise, and the effectiveness of informal or formal mentoring in promoting undergraduate academic success is assumed rather than demonstrated" (p. 526). This chapter refutes that claim, outlining the considerations and tools needed to develop an identity-conscious, peer-to-peer mentoring program and, furthermore, provides metrics to demonstrate student success.

This chapter provides a brief overview of the frameworks that support the development of an identity-conscious, peer-to-peer mentoring program and includes all details related to creating a program from scratch, including the recruitment and hiring of peer mentors, developing a training program, providing outreach to participants, and creating a retention and persistence database to demonstrate student success. Finally, the chapter concludes with five action items to create a program on your campus.

Chapter Framework

Student retention in higher education is complex. Over the past 30 years, one main criticism among higher education researchers is the lack of empirical evidence on how retention programs specifically contribute to lower attrition rates. Many qualitative studies were designed to create more empirical evidence; however, researchers are still calling for more quantitative data. Over the past five years, attrition rates for first-generation students, low-income students, and students of color remain the same as they were 30 years ago, if not worse. As a result, researchers have gathered more empirical data to help increase retention for first-generation students, low-income students, and students of color. The first focus of this literature review is to provide the latest empirical research on how first-year programs improve persistence for first-generation students, low-income students, and students of color. The second focus is to show how social integration and empowerment prove to be effective to increase persistence among these students.

Empirical data on persistence for first-generation students, low-income students, and students of color in higher education have flourished over the past five to 10 years. Studies show that first-year programs are critical to helping at-risk students persist toward graduation (Amaury & Crisp, 2007; Noble, Flynn, Lee, & Hilton, 2007). Today, these students need to be provided with networks beyond their families and friends to help them through their first year (Tierney, 1999; Wells, 2009; Zurita, 2005). First-year programs build an empowering community necessary for these students to persist and to relieve them of academic stress (Rayle & Chung, 2007). University administrators must continue to find ways to build programs and services to help first-generation students, low-income students, and students of color achieve a smooth social integration into university culture (Smith, 2005; Swail, 2003).

Tinto's (1988) early research provides a framework that focuses on social integration and creating safe spaces where students connect their life experiences to university culture (i.e., academic and social aspects of a university). It is critical for first-generation students, low-income students, and students of color to connect their life experiences with what they learn from staff, faculty, and peers so they will be more likely to persist through college. Higher education researchers declared that first-generation students, low-income students, and students of color have higher levels of attrition in universities when compared to White students. Swail (2003) provided a new geometrical integration model to increase student persistence with this student population. According to Swail, "The purpose of this model is to provide a user-friendly method for discussion and to focus on the cognitive and social attributes that the student brings to campus, and the institutional role in the student experience" (p. 76). Swail names three forces contributing to higher attrition rates for first-generation students, low-income students, and students of color: cognitive, social, and institutional. He argues that if these students do not achieve a geometrical equilibrium on these forces, they will not persist in higher education: "This model works to help describe the persistence process and the delicate balance between student resources and institutional resources" (p. 87).

Despite the severe underdevelopment of the mentoring literature, the value of mentoring has long been accepted in the literature as well as in practice (Cohen, 1993). In turn, mentoring has become a national priority (Girves, Zepeda, & Gwathmey, 2005), as demonstrated by the hundreds of formalized programs and institutional practices at the national, state, and local levels that include a mentoring component. Although the mentoring literature appears to have steadily progressed, it has lagged behind program development and implementation efforts and has yet to adequately resolve the issues broached 25 years ago by Jacobi (1991). Most notably, it appears that mentoring research has made little progress in identifying and implementing a consistent definition and conceptualization of *mentoring*, is largely atheoretical, and is lacking in terms of rigorous quantitative research designs that allow testing the external validity of findings. Therefore, an updated review of the literature on mentoring is needed to provide guidance to faculty, institutional researchers, and student affairs personnel in the development, evaluation, and analysis of future mentoring research. Although this chapter does not provide a thoroughly updated literature review, this overview provides context and support for creating a mentoring program and all the details to implement one on your campus.

Identity Consciousness

Whether you are creating an identity-conscious, peer-to-peer mentoring program to address retention and persistence because you feel called to do so, or institutional leadership has asked you to create one, be specific about what it means for your program to be identity conscious. The peer-to-peer mentoring program outlined in this chapter addresses three different and often intersecting identities. First, students of color are the main focus of this mentoring program because of the unique challenges they face at historically and predominantly White colleges and universities. Second, racial consciousness must be considered during the hiring process and training of peer mentors because it influences outreach to your target population. Third, social class and students who are the first in their family to attend college are also important identities in this program because we know that low-income students and first-generation college students are represented in higher numbers among students of color. While this may not be the case at your institution, institutional data can determine if these intersections exist for your student population. In addition to anecdotal information about the experience of students of color on college campuses, merely looking at retention, persistence, and graduation rates disaggregated by race shows students of color are not achieving these milestones at the same rates as their White peers.

This chapter is divided into three main sections: building a mentoring program, supporting systems, and tracking and reporting student success. Building a mentoring program covers strategy and purpose; recruitment, hiring, and training of peer mentors; marketing the program; and outreach to participants. Supporting systems includes sections on database needs, session reporting, and critical incident protocol. Finally, tracking and reporting student success considers how to do this given your specific institutional needs and provides tips to access information to help you understand your student population.

Building a Mentoring Program

Various components should be considered when building a program from the ground up. If you are starting at the beginning, read each section in the order presented as each subsection builds on the next. If you are enhancing or revamping an existing program, feel free to jump to the section most relevant to your immediate needs.

Strategy and Purpose

One of the most important steps in designing any program is to set clear objectives. For the purposes of this chapter, identity-conscious peer-to-peer mentoring has been selected as a tool to increase first- to second-year retention of students of color, first-generation college students, and low-income students. Formal peer-to-peer mentoring provides a high level of account-ability outside a hierarchical relationship. The program described in this chapter has the following specific outcomes:

- Increases first- to second-year retention for students of color
- Increases four- and six-year graduation rates for students of color
- Increases the percentage of students of color meeting the first-year student success metric of 48 credit hours and a 2.5 grade point average (GPA)

Methods to assess these specific objectives are discussed later. As you design your program, start with one to three main objectives. The objectives you set along with the evaluation or assessment of those objectives will frame the design and delivery of your program.

Recruitment, Hiring, and Training of Peer Mentors

The core of a strong mentoring program is the mentor staff, so take some time to write down the ideal job responsibilities. You may find that in the beginning you cannot create the ideal position and need to start small, but dream big from the inception of your program anyway. How many hours a week do you expect mentors to work? How many mentees do you antici-pate serving? How often will mentors meet with their mentees? A clear job description will aid in your recruitment (see Appendix 3.A on p. 58 for an example). Next, decide how many mentors you want to hire for your pro-gram. Depending on your campus environment, you should aim for double the number of applicants for the number of positions you set. It's always a good idea to maintain a deep applicant pool.

Ideally, if you would like the mentors to start in the fall, start the recruitment and hiring process in January of that year. This will allow you to hire mentors as well as coordinate a few meet-and-greet or training ses-sions before students leave for the summer. Be sure to determine and include important dates in your application and onboarding process so students know what to expect if they are hired. Additionally, you may want to set a predeter-mined staff meeting day and time. In the past few years of hiring a peer men-tor staff of 35 to 46 students, we have found it too challenging to try to match schedules after everyone has been hired. Instead, set students up for success and let them know the expectations regarding availability for staff meetings. If you decide that staff meetings will be on Friday from 1:00 p.m. to 3:00 p.m., students will know not to choose classes scheduled at that time and not to accept work shifts that conflict with that time. Considering the population with whom you are working, odds are high that students may have additional jobs or commitments. Hiring well in advance allows students to make scheduling adjustments.

Once you have hired your staff, shift your focus to training; determine when it will be and how long it will last. A minimum of one week is needed to cover the absolute basics. Don't try to cover every possible item before the school year starts; the staff meetings throughout the year can be used for continued professional development. Your first session, which I refer to as immersion training, should build efficacy and give student mentors everything they need to be successful in their outreach efforts and first mentee meetings. The bulk of immersion training should provide students with an opportunity to better understand their own identities and the purpose of the program and become comfortable with recruiting students. Although it is important for you to conduct sessions on the program-specific components, ask your colleagues in your department and across campus to assist in other training sessions. Doing this decreases your work. It also introduces mentors to staff members across the university, which will help them in their role as a peer mentor by giving them firsthand knowledge of the dean of students office and its functions, for example, as well as other offices and their activities. In a peer-to-peer mentoring program, student mentors can use their own experience in successfully navigating campus challenges and using various campus resources to help their student mentee. Appendix 3.B on p. 59 contains a sample training schedule.

Marketing the Program

Marketing begins before your first-year students even set foot on campus. Because your marketing efforts should begin when students are admitted to your institution, developing a relationship with admissions staff is integral. Meet with admissions staff to learn about their information queue, which is the schedule set up by admissions for sending informational materials to admitted students. An acceptance or decision letter typically goes out on the first day of the queue, and pertinent information is sent at specific subsequent intervals. The admissions staff can let you know when a welcome letter on your peer-mentoring program could be included in its regular communications with students. This is an easy way to introduce new students and their parents to your program's name and provide basic information, because parents can have an influential role in marketing your program to prospective participants.

Ask the admissions department for its first-year student information on your target population. Are you targeting students of color, first-generation students, low-income students, or all of these? If you haven't quite determined your population, your admissions staff may be helpful by providing you with the information collected from student applications and other indicators during the application process. For example, many schools have a formula that indicates or assigns the type of college preparation at students' high schools. Most admissions processes have a way to determine the level of college preparedness of potential students. This is the type of indicator you may be interested in for your program.

A call campaign should be the next phase of marketing. Direct contact with parents and incoming students can help create investment and excitement in your program. Determine if a call campaign is something you can manage in your own office or if the university has resources you can use. Schedule the call campaign over the summer. A telecommunications or teleservices department or unit on your campus can be of great assistance in this process. If you don't have access to such a service, ask yourself the following questions:

- How many households are in our target population? Will we call parents and students? Will we call them separately?
- Do we have funding to hire students to make phone calls?
- What do we want parents or students to learn from our calls?
- What is the main selling point to make before concluding the phone call?

The first two questions concern feasibility. These are the same questions your telecommunications unit would ask if it worked with you on this project. The second two questions help you create your script. You want all the phone calls to be relatively similar in content, and you want students to have a guide that details how a typical phone conversation should be conducted as well as the key information that must be transmitted during a phone conversation. In the years I've run a call campaign for peer mentoring programs, we wanted parents and students to understand the benefits of participating in the program. Featuring the most salient benefits to program participants in the phone call guide allows the caller to clearly communicate the direct value of participation to the incoming students' parents. Also, the final point of the call should be to tell students about your kickoff event, which should be scheduled for the first day of classes. The purpose of the call is not to sign up students for the program; instead, it is to provide information. But you do want them to know about the kickoff event, which is an integral component of participant outreach. One final note about call campaigns: The campaign will become easier to coordinate after the first year of the program because you can hire students who were participants and who can relate their own experiences during the phone calls.

Outreach to Participants

To begin your participant outreach, you should have already determined who is in your target population and how you're planning to make mentor/mentee assignments. Are you making assignments based on identity, where students are from, or their major or academic college? A list of names in your target group from your admissions office will allow you to preassign mentees to your mentors. At the conclusion of immersion training, each mentor receives a list of mentees he or she is responsible for contacting. If you host your immersion training the week before classes start, this gives students three to five days to contact all mentees they have been assigned. In their communications with students, mentors should identify themselves as participants in the mentoring program and as the students' assigned mentors. Mentors should focus on getting their students to the kickoff event so they can all meet and learn more about the program. If you're not having a kickoff event, mentors should focus on setting up a first meeting. Mentors should remind mentees that agreeing to a meeting of 15 to 30 minutes does not obligate them to sign up for the program. Getting students to a kickoff event can reinforce the interest that may have been building since the call campaign. It will also allow mentors the opportunity to meet several students all at one time.

Whether or not you're having a kickoff event, contact guidelines for your mentor staff are key. Typically, students will sign up or agree to participate in the program within the first three weeks. In my years running a peer mentoring program, I have found that two contact attempts per week from a mentor using two different methods seem to work well without overwhelming everyone. For example, if a mentor calls a student on Monday, he or she might want to send a follow-up e-mail on Wednesday or Thursday. If mentors use different methods of contacting students during the first three weeks, they will either get in touch with the student or not. At the end of the outreach period, provide your staff with a tracking sheet to report on their progress. This will also be helpful information for your future planning. This tracking information lets you determine the number of students who declined participation as well as those who never responded.

The final component of outreach is formalizing participation, such as a mentor-mentee agreement that outlines the expectations of the mentees as well as what they can expect from their mentors. It is a great conversation piece for the mentor and mentee as well because it allows them to discuss more thoroughly what they both hope to gain from participating in the program, and it gives mentees a good understanding of the mentor's commitment to them as individuals.

Supporting Systems

Regardless of the size of your mentor and mentee population, creating supporting systems such as a database, session reporting, and critical incident protocol are key components for accountability purposes. A database can help with assigning mentees, keeping track of demographic information, and tracking active participation in the program. Creating a session reporting process, either paper or electronic, is necessary to hold peer mentors accountable and to identify common themes discussed in mentor/mentee meetings. Finally, a critical incident protocol, key to the advocacy component of the program, provides mentors with methods to alert professional staff to critical incidents their mentees might be facing.

Database Needs

A basic database should include all data points available for each mentor and mentee. While an Excel spreadsheet may be sufficient to track information, I recommend Microsoft Access, which acts like Excel in many ways but is a bit more sophisticated. One of the biggest advantages of using Access is the ability to accommodate multiple users at one time. If more than one person needs to access the database at the same time, it is well worth the effort to learn to use Access. In addition, this software offers more query options to run demographic information on your active and inactive populations.

Determine the kind of information you want to analyze about your population, such as college representation, race, sex, first-generation status, and so on. You should be able to run the entire program with the information in the database. In your first year, you may decide to keep your database more basic. As your program grows and you go through a full-year cycle or more, you'll have a better sense of the information you need and the types of queries you're interested in running. I have used the program database to assign mentees and keep track of who becomes active and who doesn't. With the database, I can always produce accurate reports on population being served and basic demographics of those included in the population. Because my database has always held the entire target population, including all the students who choose not to participate in the program, I am able to produce reports that clearly show the percentage of each target population that opted to participate in the program. You should expect your database to evolve as your program does over the course of a single year and over the course of several years.

Session Reporting

You or your supervisor will probably be interested in confirming that mentors are meeting with their mentees. The answer is session reports, which are completed by mentors after each meeting with a mentee. The report asks some basic information: who, when, how long, and what type of meeting (in person, phone, virtual communication). You may also be interested in the type of issues discussed during the meeting, so provide a few checkboxes for issue items such as transition, social, financial, academic, or personal. It is important to also provide space for mentors to describe the meeting, giving feedback on questions such as how the student is doing, what the mentor and mentee discussed, and if there is anything of critical concern about which the supervisor needs to know. (The point about critical concern is discussed more thoroughly in the next section.) Finally, you may include a section for mentors to include any questions they may have for their supervisor.

Once you have determined the information you'd like to gather from session reports, determine the method of collection. If you are just starting out, you may ask mentors to turn in hard-copy reports. If possible, explore electronic options for session reports to streamline the process for you and your staff. If mentors are able to submit reports online, they are more likely to write reports immediately following meetings instead of waiting until they have to submit them in person at staff meetings, for example. An electronic option will also allow the supervisor to manage reviewing reports. If you receive them all at once, you may be more inclined to read them all at once, and depending on the size of your active student population, you could be reading hundreds of reports at one time. Online submission can provide more opportunities to review a certain amount per day or maybe review a certain group of staff members' reports throughout the week. Either way, it is important to not only create the session report or due dates for staff members but also consider when the supervisor will review the reports.

Critical Incident Protocol

A critical incident protocol is imperative for a peer-to-peer mentoring program used as a retention initiative. For the sake of this chapter, a *critical incident* is defined as any issue that would prevent a student from remaining at your institution. Therefore, this could include issues such as a financial aid hold on a student's account for lack of timely tuition payment, a roommate conflict, or a student pregnancy. You will soon discover the typical incidents for your own student population. It's important to distinguish between a critical incident and an emergency situation. Critical incident protocol should not replace any already existing emergency protocol for your students. If something is an emergency situation, mentors and mentees should contact campus police or call 911 for immediate response. Because critical incidents can quickly lead to student attrition, it's important to implement a protocol that has the quickest response.

If you have an electronic session reporting process, decide if the report should include a critical incident section and a mechanism to alert the supervisor. Even if you don't have an electronic reporting system, the following critical incident protocol is useful.

1. Mentor identifies a critical incident. This can come to light during a regularly scheduled meeting or by a mentee notifying his or her mentor.
2. Mentor submits a session report outline with all the information gathered from the student. After submitting the report, the mentor should contact the supervisor to tell him or her that a critical incident report has been submitted.

You may decide to let your mentors submit a critical incident report in a different format; for example, an e-mail might be more expeditious for the overall process. As a supervisor, you may want to directly contact the student to meet in person and gather more information, or you may decide you need to chat with the mentor first.

As you begin to identify the more typical critical incidents for your student population, you may enhance this protocol. For example, financial aid holds or outstanding bills made up the majority of the critical incidents in my student populations, so I added several steps to the process. First, mentors were given a few typical questions to ask their mentees, such as asking if they completed their student loan entrance counseling, and are they registered for the appropriate number of class credits? These questions allow mentors to help mentees with their concerns, thereby decreasing the number of students a supervisor may need to contact. For more advanced financial issues, mentors should tell mentees to schedule a meeting with the supervisor and provide them with instructions on how to do so. Some mentors might even walk their students to the office to schedule the meeting right away. This is just one example of how you might enhance the critical incident protocol based on your student population and typical critical incidents. Overall, keep the reporting process simple for your mentor staff.

Assessment: How Do You Know It Works?

As previously mentioned, determining program objectives in addition to student success are the first steps in the process of creating a peer-to-peer mentoring program. Matching this metric of success to your university's metrics is a key strategic element. If you're hoping to make comparisons between your active and inactive populations or make comparisons to the university's metrics, you'll need to match these metrics of success. Your office of institutional research can provide more information about this. Regardless of the size of your institution, at least one person is tracking retention and persistence for the institution as a whole, officially or unofficially. Often the number of credit hours attained and GPA are used in measuring this. If your institution doesn't track this information, it would be useful to determine what is necessary for first-year students to be able to graduate in four years (or five years if that is better aligned with your institution). Beyond the first- to second-year transition and a student success metric, you may decide to also track graduation rates. Understanding what your institution already tracks can help provide a road map for you to decide what to track for your participant group.

If you do not have institutional data for comparison, look at your target population. How did students who chose to participate fare against the students in your target population who did not participate? Depending on your target population, you may track success comprehensively or by specific identity groups. For example, you may choose to compare active and inactive students by race to provide a more similar comparison, which can provide a more nuanced picture of your students as well. Often, your overall comparison may not show a huge difference for active and inactive students, but a breakdown by race or first-generation status may show greater success for your student participants versus their comparative peers who did not participate. Aside from having institutional data for comparison, providing a clear rationale for your definition of *success* is key to grounding your tracking and reporting methods.

To determine specific methods to measure success, the following objectives and metrics are suggested:

- Increase first- to second-year retention for students of color. Because this program targeted first-year students of color, this objective is measured by comparing the retention rate for active participants with those who chose not to participate. Over the course of three years, we saw an increase in the gap between active and inactive participants from 9% to 16%; that is, students who participated in the program were 16% more likely to be retained than their like peers.
- Increase the percentage of students of color meeting the first-year student success metric of 48 credit hours and a 2.5 GPA. This university used a first-year student success metric of 48 credit hours attained and a 2.5 GPA. After reviewing several years of data, the university determined this metric because first-year students who hit

this mark were most likely to graduate in four years. This metric was also broken down by race to provide the most similar comparison. Over the course of three years, African American student participants were 20% more likely to hit this metric than nonparticipants of the same racial identity.

- Increase four- and six-year graduation rates for students of color. Although this is specifically a first-year program, research shows that students who are retained after their first year contribute to the university's four- and six-year graduation rates. To provide a more accurate comparison, this data is broken down by race. Although the difference between the four-year graduation rate for African American active participants and for African American nonparticipants was only 2%, the five-year graduation rates for African American students show a 13% difference between active participants and nonparticipants.

These examples provide a template for using your program objectives to determine your assessment metrics and thus prove that your program is accomplishing what it set out to do.

The information in this chapter provides you with everything you need to design and launch an identity-conscious peer-to-peer mentoring program. The mentor staff is the lifeblood of the program; therefore, attention should be paid to recruiting, hiring, and training a staff that can tend to the unique needs and identities in your target audience. Even if you are not pairing mentors and mentees by identity, you'll want a staff that represents the diversity of your participants. Additionally, this program is identity conscious because of the special attention placed on training staff to equip them to mentor and build relationships across difference. Mentors who understand the institutional and systemic barriers for students of color, first-generation college students, and low-income students are the best ambassadors of the program and are also able to explain the benefits of participating to prospective mentees.

Supporting systems allow you to run an efficient program that can serve many participants. A peer-to-peer mentoring program of this caliber can be scaled up to serve hundreds and thousands of students but only if you incorporate important structures such as a database, session reporting, and a critical incident protocol. These systems allow you to assign mentees to mentors, track participation, and hold mentors accountable. These systems also help with quick response to critical incidents and enable information sharing when necessary. Finally, publicizing the success of the program broadly lies in tracking and reporting student success metrics such as retention, credit hours attained, and GPA. You must have a method to present your outcomes to ensure sustainability of the program.

Conclusion

First- to second-year retention is at the core of the persistence and graduation conversation. If students are not being retained after their first year, persistence and graduation are irrelevant. After all, if they are not retained in their first year, they are not persisting and certainly cannot graduate from your institution. We can expect a certain amount of attrition each year. Students may choose to transfer because they have changed their major, they need to be closer to home, or for various other reasons that may not be attributed to the institution at all. This is to be expected but at equal rates across identity. If traditionally marginalized student populations are not being retained or are failing to attain success metrics at drastically higher rates than their privileged peers, this is a problem that needs to be addressed. I cannot say if an identity-conscious peer-to-peer mentoring program is the solution for your campus, but increasing first- to second-year retention is the first place to start.

If your institution's administrators have noticed that graduation rates for students of color are dramatically different than those of White students, the first- to second-year transition should be the first place to investigate. The first- to second-year retention rate may be actually fine and maybe the university is losing students at a different point in their college career. If this is the case, other chapters in this book may help you identify and address the problem. Use your institutional data to build your intervention. Don't be afraid to disaggregate by race, socioeconomic status, and first-generation status. Are students with intersecting identities experiencing even greater risk? If you have limited funds, this intersectional area this could be the best place to start. Documented success with a smaller population of students can assist in obtaining funds to expand the scope of the program. We cannot ignore the logical progression of a student's academic career. If students aren't retained, they cannot persist and, therefore, cannot graduate.

Action Items

- Collect data. Why do you need this program? In particular, look at your first- to second-year retention rates by race. If students of color are not being retained at the same rates as White students, this program can help. Also, beyond retention, find out what your institution uses to determine success in the first year. Often, this is a combination of credit hours and GPA. Connecting with a colleague in your institutional research office could be helpful. Again, be sure to compare these data based on the identities your program targets (race, social class, first-generation status.)

- Assess and assemble stakeholders. Who on your campus can support you in developing this initiative? Look to your admissions office, the gatekeeper of student demographic information. Without a clear commitment to partnerships, it may be challenging to get this program off the ground. Who else on your campus will be key supporters?
- Determine your scope and budget. How many students are in your target audience? Are they all students of color or students of color who are also first-generation college students? The number of students you intend to contact can determine how many mentors you hire. Scope and budget go hand in hand. How many mentors can you hire related to the number of students you can realistically serve? A good formula for this is one mentor (at 10 hours of work per week) to support 15 students maximum. You can assume a 50% participation rate from your target audience. For example, if your target audience is 300 students, roughly 150 will actively participate in the program. Therefore you need to hire at least 10 mentors.

References

Amaury, N., & Crisp, G. (2007). Mentoring students: Conceptualizing and validating the multi-dimensions of a support system. *Journal of College Student Retention*, *9*(3), 337–356.

Cohen, N. H. (1993). *The development and validation of the principles of adult mentoring scale for faculty mentoring in higher education* (Unpublished doctoral dissertation). Temple University, Philadelphia, PA.

Girves, J. E., Zepeda, Y., & Gwathmey, J. K. (2005). Mentoring in a post-affirmative action world. *Journal of Social Issues*, *61*(3), 449–480.

Jacobi, M. (1991). Mentoring and undergraduate academic success: A literature review. *Review of Educational Research*, *61*(4), 505–532.

Noble, K., Flynn, N., Lee, J. D., & Hilton, D. (2007). Predicting successful college experiences: Evidence from a first year retention program. *Journal of College Student Retention*, *9*(1), 39–60.

Ragins, B. R., & Cotton, J. (1999). Mentor functions and outcomes: A comparison of men and women in formal and informal mentoring relationships. *Journal of Applied Psychology*, *84*(4), 529–550.

Rayle, A. D., & Chung, K. Y., (2007). Revisiting first-year college students' mattering: Social support, academic stress, and the mattering experience. *Journal of College Student Retention*, *9*(1), 21–37.

Seibert, S. (1999). The effectiveness of facilitated mentoring: A longitudinal quasi-experiment. *Journal of Vocational Behavior*, *54*(3), 483–502.

Smith, J. S. (2005). The effects of student receptivity on college achievement and retention. *Journal of College Student Retention*, *6*(3), 273–288.

Swail, W. (2003). *Retaining minority students in higher education: A framework for success.* San Francisco: CA: Jossey-Bass.

Tierney, W. G., (1999). Models of minority college-going and retention: Cultural integrity versus cultural suicide. *Journal of Negro Education, 68*(1), 80–91.

Tinto, V. (1988). Stages of student departure: Reflections on the longitudinal character of student leaving. *Journal of Higher Education, 59*(4), 438–455.

Upcraft. M. L. & Gardner, J. N. (1989). *The freshman year experience.* San Francisco. CA: Jossey-Bass.

Wells, R. (2009). Social and cultural capital, race and ethnicity, and college student retention. *Journal of College Student Retention, 10*(2), 103–128.

Zurita, M. (2005). Stopping out and persisting: Experiences of Latino undergraduates. *Journal of College Student Retention, 6*(3), 301–324.

Appendix 3.A

Peer Mentor: Sample Job Description

General Summary: A peer mentor serves as an academic mentor, an advocate, and a resource for 10 to 15 students who are assigned to him or her as mentees. The mentees are first-year students who are either the first in their families to go to college, are from low-income families, or are students of color. The mentoring relationship lasts the entire year, and the peer mentors must meet with each of their mentees every other week and attend a weekly two-hour staff meeting. A peer mentor should be looking for leadership development, one-on-one work with higher risk college students, and ongoing engagement with issues of social justice and diversity.

Time Percentages for Principle Duties and Responsibilities, and Other Job-Related Information

1. 40%: Serve as a peer mentor to 10 to 15 incoming first-year students while identifying and addressing the specific needs of students of color, making referrals when appropriate.
2. 25%: Develop, coordinate, and implement logistics for social and academic activities, programs, events, and presentations on and off campus.
3. 10%: Attend and actively contribute to all weekly staff meetings and maintain weekly contact with the peer mentoring program leadership team through written reports.
4. 10%: Maintain regular (in person, e-mail, or phone) communication with the cohort of designated mentees
5. 10%: Participate in required training sessions and orientations (may include some evenings and weekends).
6. 5%: Perform other duties as assigned.

Position Requirements

Minimum Knowledge, Skills, and Abilities

1. Excellent interpersonal/customer service skills
2. Ability to organize, file, and maintain office documents
3. Ability to multitask and work in a fast-paced environment
4. Appreciation for diversity
5. Proficiency in Microsoft Word, Excel, PowerPoint, and Outlook
6. A clear understanding of and commitment to addressing issues affecting students of color, first-generation college students, and low-income students

Qualifications

1. Commitment to academic excellence, demonstrated by maintaining a GPA of 2.5 or above
2. Knowledge of university resources and services
3. Excellent oral and written communication skills
4. Cannot hold other campus leadership positions that conflict with peer mentor training and duties

Hours/Schedule

The peer mentor should be available for work 10 hours per week including some evening and weekend hours. The peer mentor must be willing to commit to the position for one academic year pending quarterly evaluations. Compensation for the position is a $2,750 stipend, disbursed biweekly throughout the academic year.

Peer mentors must be available to attend a weeklong paid training session the week prior to the start of the school year.

Appendix 3.B

Sample Peer Mentor Training Schedule

Tuesday, September 3, 2013 Training Location: Arts & Letters 410–412 Curricular Theme: Introduction to Peer Mentoring		
Time	*Activity*	*Facilitator*
9:00 a.m.–10 a.m.	Welcome and Training Overview Expectations	Sara
10:00 a.m.–11 a.m.	Career Center Paperwork Session	Office of Student Employment
11:00 a.m.– 12:00 p.m.	Surprise!	Super Surprise!
12:00 p.m.–1:00 p.m.	Office of Multicultural Student Success Overview and Lunch	Vijay
1:00 p.m.–1:30 p.m.	Departmental Expectations	Sara
1:30 p.m.–3:00 p.m.	Goal Setting Personal Accountability	Chris
3:00 p.m.–4:00 p.m.	Time After Time Management	Andrea
4:00 p.m.–5:00 p.m.	What Do I Want for My Mentees? What Am I Willing to Do to Ensure Their Success?	Sara

Wednesday, September 4, 2013 Training Location: Arts & Letters Hall 410–412 Curricular Theme: Establishing the Program Context		
Time	*Activity*	*Facilitator*
9:00 a.m.–10:00 a.m.	Welcome and Energizer	Chris
10:00 a.m.–12:30 p.m.	Social Justice League, Part I	Shanika
12:30 p.m.–1:30 p.m.	Lunch	
1:30 p.m.–3:00 p.m.	Staff Meetings Overview Group Accountability	Sara
3:00 p.m.–4:00 p.m.	What Does It Mean to Be Part of This Mentoring Program? • Outreach Expectations	Chris
4:00 p.m.–5:00 p.m.	Call Me Maybe?	Sara

Thursday, September 5, 2013 Training Location: Arts & Letters Hall 410–412 Curricular Theme: Who Am I?		
Time	*Activity*	*Facilitator*
9:00 a.m.–10:00 a.m.	Welcome and Energizer	Chris
10:00 a.m.–12:00 p.m.	Social Justice League, Part II	Shanika
12:00 p.m.–1:00 p.m.	Lunch	
1:00 p. m.–3:30 p.m.	Kick Off Event Mentee List	Sara
3:30 p.m.–5:00 p.m.	Professional Staff/Graduate Assistant Mingle	Chris

Friday, September 6, 2013 Arts & Letters Hall 410–412 Curricular Theme: Who Are We?		
Time	*Activity*	*Facilitator*
9:00 a.m.–9:50 a.m.	Welcome, Settle In, Energizer	Chris
10:00 a.m.–10:30 a.m.	It's That Time Again . . .	Andrea
10:30 a.m.– 11:30 a.m.	Programming Overview • Expectations • Points Overview	Chris
11:30 a.m.–12:00 p.m.	Critical Incident Overview	Sara
12:00 p.m.–1:00 p.m.	Lunch and Break	
1:00 p.m.–3:00 p.m.	Advocacy Panel	Sara
3:00 p.m.–4:30 p.m.	Technology/Communication Overview • Session Reporting • Social Media • Newsletter	Chris Kat Wesley
4:30 p.m.–5:00 p.m.	Things That Make You Go Hmm . . .	Sara

Monday, September 9, 2013 Training Location: Irons Oaks Challenge Course Curricular Theme: Who Are We in Community?		
Time	*Activity*	*Facilitator*
8:30 a.m. –9:30 a.m.	Meet at the Egan Statue • Buses Will Depart on Time!	Sara
9:30 a.m.–12:00 p.m.	Arrive at Irons Oaks: Challenge Course!	
12:00 p.m.–3:30 p.m.	Lunch	
3:30 p.m.–5:00 p.m.	Group Picture and Depart for Campus	
5:00 p.m.	Return to Lincoln Park	

4

THE PROMISE AND CHALLENGE OF LEADERSHIP DEVELOPMENT FOR WOMEN OF COLOR

Tomika Rodriguez

Many women of color stopped by my office in the blur of October 2011 after the tragic murder of a promising, smart, driven man of color on campus. He was a prominent member of my institution's Men of Color Initiative, and his death sent shockwaves through the student community. Many of the women who came to see me after his death were also promising, smart, and driven, and they candidly told me of the challenge of contending with their—and our—loss, with some struggling to reconcile their faith with their new reality. In the coming weeks and months, I and many of my colleagues worked to support students as they grieved. As the coordinator for my institution's women of color leadership program, Women Empowered (WE), I in particular spent countless hours with many of our young women of color. As noted in Sinclair-Chapman, Eloi, and King's (2014) account of creating the Women of Color Circle, this anecdote represents a powerful example of a community attempting to "fill a void in [supporting women of color's academic and social care" (p. 219). I chose to begin this chapter on leadership development for women of color in college with this particular anecdote because I believe that their search for meaning and resolve in the face of a crisis points to the necessity and relevance of using an identity-conscious framework to engage women of color in developing their leadership capacity, including their capacity for resilience, renewal, and positive action.

Overview

In 2009, I created the WE program, a leadership development program for college students who are women of color. When advertising the program to students, and later during conference presentations, I shared a question I'd heard posed during the Democratic primary of the 2008 presidential election. With Senator Hillary Rodham Clinton and Senator Barack Obama up for nomination, would female Democrats of color vote their race or vote their gender? Although this question was not an impetus for the program and not relevant to all women of color, its framing helps to illuminate the challenge facing higher education professionals charged with developing student leadership programs for women of color with their multiple and intersecting identities.

Women of color by definition have two marginalized social identities: a gender that has collectively experienced patriarchal oppression and a racial minority that has collectively experienced systemic racism. Although not monolithic, women of color's common cultural identity (largely defined by their outsider status) is the result of belonging to both those marginalized groups and the interplay between them. Martínez Alemán (2000) describes race and gender as "fluid, dynamic, and interrelated; suggesting that to understand the experiences of women of color requires an [acknowledgment] . . . that at no particular moment are these women solely one thing or another" (p. 145). Higher education professionals who have an understanding of women of color's cultural identity are better able to help them address their lived experiences.

Each of these marginalized identities and their convergence result in particular inequities for women of color in society. For certain groups, including women and girls of color, an *opportunity gap*, which is defined as "the ways in which race, ethnicity, socioeconomic status, English proficiency, community wealth, familial situations, or other factors contribute to or perpetuate lower educational aspirations, achievement, and attainment" ("Opportunity Gap," 2013, para. 1), persists. Women of color are not fine on a number of economic, health, and educational indicators, and largely remain missing from the retention and success literature in higher education and, further, in the national discourse on issues of identity-based justice.

The politics of the intersection of race and gender have come into stark relief. The White House Council on Women and Girls (2014) released a report detailing the promise and challenge for women of color and girls and announcing the formation of a working group to focus on issues "including education, economic security, health, criminal and juvenile justice, violence, and research and data collection" (p. 2). This is a welcome initiative and may have many implications, including an increased focus on educational equity for women and girls of color. In the report, President Obama argues that we underestimate the complexity of the challenges faced by women of color in American society. The report adds that "a high-quality education is no longer just a pathway to opportunity—it is a prerequisite for success" (p. 8). In concert with this clarion call from the White House, I propose in this chapter that a growing responsibility for higher education is to meaningfully invest in the student success of women of color who seek higher education. If the highest office in the nation can correct course by turning a critical eye to examine and address barriers and disparities uniquely faced by women of color, then so too can higher education.

By prioritizing the growing call for an explicit focus on student success, this chapter describes the importance of taking an identity-conscious approach to leadership development for women of color, expanded here to include explicitly preparing students for personal, academic, and postcollege success, which requires supporting the development of attitudes and behaviors needed to integrate leadership as a personal identity and equipping students with a tool kit to refine and sustain that identity. The following section highlights a blended theoretical framework that can be used to create and deliver women of color leadership programs (WOCLPs), outlines a successful curriculum that defines a clear path for creating a leadership development program for women of color, and concludes with recommendations for those who want to launch programs at their own institutions.

Chapter Framework

Leadership development has come to be regarded as an important higher education outcome, with an increasing emphasis on empowering students "to clarify personal values and interests, . . . experience diverse peers, learn about self, and develop new skills" (Komives, Owen, Longerbeam, Mainella, & Osteen, 2005, p. 598). With a society that is ever growing in number and diversity, it is important to provide students with an attainable set of success skills that also takes account of their individual and collective circumstances, histories, and goals. Scholars deservedly remain critical of leadership frameworks that still rely on old practices to offer a one-size-fits-all approach to assist students in acquiring a leadership identity and even find that developing research "seems to mirror the broader leadership studies literature in its colorblind approach" (Dugan, Kodama, & Gebhardt, 2012, p. 174). The program outlined in this chapter integrates theoretical frameworks that help students adopt a leadership identity and acknowledges and supports them in developing their unique and intersecting social identities.

Leadership identity development (LID) is an emerging but prominent model that stresses "shifting from an external view of leadership to leadership as a process" (Komives et al., 2005, p. 605), with students ultimately considering leadership an integral part of their own personal and healthy self-concept, regardless of their role or position. LID represents an important evolution in leadership studies, but, like its predecessors, it does not take the additional step of integrating social identity development. Kodama and Dugan (2013) cite researchers who situate identity-based organizations as "a key source of leadership development for students of color," and conclude they "may be a particularly powerful venue" (p. 194) in a discussion of expanded spaces and activities that can lend themselves to developing a leadership identity (Kodama & Dugan, 2013; Renn & Ozaki, 2010). For women of color, these efforts can be enhanced by using an intersectional lens to build leadership development programs.

Intersectionality, a theory that has long explored gender as it intersects with other dimensions of social identity (Shields, 2008), is a useful lens for programs that prepare women of color to bring their strengths to the fore; acknowledge and embrace diverse perspectives; and navigate barriers to personal, academic, and professional success. Intersectionality is concerned with "both the external work of social change as well as the personal work of understanding one's own identity" (Jennrich & Kowalski-Braun, 2014, p. 203). As we learn from a foundational study on the model of multiple dimensions of identity (MMDI) theory, which builds on intersectionality theory, multiple identities are constantly at play, with women describing a core or "inside" identity versus "outside" social identities (Jones & McEwen, 2000, p. 408). Although outside social identities are considered less meaningful by study participants, we know they can structure a generalized understanding of an individual's opportunities in life, including the quality of education one obtains as well as the difficulty in doing so. Using MMDI theory as a guide to help develop a core identity for women of color is a promising student development practice that makes intersectionality more accessible and issues a directive to higher education professionals to apply emerging theories in support of developing women of color as leaders.

Finally, an important framework borrowed from other disciplines like social work and youth development is empowerment as a leadership development strategy that engenders agency. It is my belief that issues of agency and empowerment have significant implications for identity-conscious leadership development programs in higher education, and the WE program relied on the framework to help participants embark upon the process of finding "power within . . . power with . . . and power to" (Hur, 2006, p. 529). To centralize empowerment as a concept, I have used an evaluative tool built on personal empowerment for women, with *empowerment* defined as a process that enables women to access skills and resources to effectively cope with current and future stress and, in effect, develop skills to sustain a leadership identity. This tool is explored in a discussion of program assessment later in this chapter.

Identity Consciousness

Current identity-centered or identity-neutral experiences in higher education may miss opportunities to foster success outcomes for women of color. Leadership development can aptly be described as student success programming, with Dugan and colleagues (2012) finding that

> scholars have linked gains in leadership capacity to other critical college outcomes, including academic persistence, career aspirations, academic and work-related performance, the ability to combat stereotype threat, and adaptability. . . . [These are] capacities which may be especially relevant for students of color attempting to navigate institutional and societal structures designed to systematically privilege and oppress. (p. 175)

However, for women of color, the absence of identity development is often a missing link, which can be "especially relevant because it influences our sense of self in regard to capabilities, motivations, and goals, all of which influence capacity for leadership" (Vasquez & Comas-Díaz, 2007, p. 268).

Similarly, the literature on fostering peer relationships for women indicate positive, if noninstitutionalized, effects on a woman of color. These include increased self-esteem, increased leadership development, enhanced feelings of mattering, and expanded access to broader campus engagement (Jackson, 1998; Kezar & Moriarty, 2000; Renn & Ozaki, 2010). These existing efforts to create and foster positive spaces through student organizations or resource groups is an important effort toward supporting women of color in higher education, but the program outlined in this chapter builds on those efforts and advocates for new, intentional, and expanded strategies to increase retention and success outcomes for women of color. It illustrates an emerging practice of integrating social and leadership identity development to not only recognize the significance of identity-centered social experiences but also take an identity-conscious approach to building a program designed to increase leadership capacity in women of color. It puts race and gender at the center of a student's leadership development journey, takes into account societal influences, and challenges the institution to go beyond "the default function . . . of center[ing] the experiences of dominant groups without naming it as such" (Linder & Rodriguez, 2012 p. 396).

Building a Leadership Curriculum Centered on Women of Color

According to scholar Chandra Talpade Mohanty,

> Race, class, gender and nation are all relational categories. They're all about relationships. They are not things that are embedded in you. So race is not something that is embedded in brown people. Gender is not something that is embedded in women. Gender is about relationships among and between men and women, women and women, women of different classes, men and men. It's about all those things. (as cited in Nguyen, 2009, p. 82)

In trying to center the experience of a marginalized group, I caution that these women are unified by characteristics beyond their control. Although this chapter presents a model and curriculum for engaging women of color in leadership development, the resulting solution is a program that bands together women from distinct racial or ethnic communities who are tacitly unified by cultural commonalities that are in response to their socially constructed outside identities. It's not without its challenges, and it must be taken for granted that in this chapter, at times, I generalize as a means of identifying patterns and commonalities for women of color but I also offer a resource-sensitive first step toward identity-conscious leadership development for women of color.

In the years I spent running the WE program, we offered a unique opportunity for college women of color to participate in an empowerment initiative through a year-long experience that used a cohort model. The cohort model allowed the WE program to build a rich, successful, and enjoyable community and included dedicated undergraduate and graduate student employees and volunteers, themselves women of color, who, along with myself, made up the program staff. The following sections outline how the program staff engaged participants throughout their year-long experience, the goals and learning outcomes we hoped the program and participants would achieve, and details of the elements of the program. Then, this section concludes with a brief discussion of program assessment.

Program Design

The program welcomes juniors and seniors to the cohort to allow first-year students to focus on their transition into campus life and to acknowledge the sensitivity and developmental readiness upper-class women may need to explore their own personal identities and to make the cognitive and intentional switch to view them through an intersectional lens. Students who identify as women of color can join the program in the final term of their freshman year through the final term of their junior year, embarking on the year-long experience the following academic year.

Joining season is so named because the enrollment process is not intended to perpetuate the legacy of exclusion women of color have often faced in higher education; students do not apply for the program, they join it, and best efforts should be made to accommodate the number of interested women. Students complete a form that captures demographic information; respond to short-answer questions on their interest in cohort membership; indicate they understand the nature of the program as an intensive, active leadership opportunity; and affirm their commitment to the bimonthly meetings and predetermined program calendar dates. Bimonthly meetings should be scheduled consistently on the same day of the week to give students a more complete understanding of their expected involvement and the opportunity to balance the program with their many commitments. Along these lines, any WOCLP should be constructed so that it is not isolated from other departmental efforts. Working collaboratively with program managers to support students' participation across multiple programs can be efficient and can expose your participants to the best developmental experiences in other units.

Program Goals

WE has the following program goals:

- to build coalitions between and among women of color;
- to provide directed support for women of color to perform at their highest potential in various personal, academic, and other leadership spheres;
- to centralize existing resources by tapping into the expertise of women of color faculty, staff, and allies across the university community and beyond to support success, development, and retention of women of color; and
- to provide a safe space for intragroup and, where relevant, intergroup dialogue and development.

Learning Outcomes

As a result of their participation in an identity-conscious leadership development program, students are expected to be able to

- practice successful strategies for effective self-care,
- demonstrate effective decision making related to personal financial management,

- demonstrate skills to construct a career plan toward postcollege career success,
- integrate personal values with the socially responsible leadership (SRL) model, and
- demonstrate characteristics of a healthy self-concept.

In a program charged with success outcomes, it is essential for learning outcomes to emphasize leadership readiness for participants, but leadership frameworks rarely take into account the physical, mental, social, and emotional well-being of the leader herself. With gendered expectations of nurturing others and a cultural emphasis on collectivity, an all-too-true cliché is that women of color may find it particularly difficult to prioritize their own sense of well-being. Owen, Komives, Lucas, and McMahon (2007) describe personal renewal as "an essential task of leadership" (p. 6) and identify practicing reflection, seeking balance, and maintaining healthy practices as important renewal skills to develop. Naming these as significant learning outcomes and exploring means for achieving them are some best practices for centering the needs of women of color and can be tools for their success in leadership development programming.

Another learning outcome that can be uniquely attained through WOCLP is related to socially responsible leadership, interpreted as applying lessons learned to positively affect the lives of others. This incorporates the empowerment practice of mobilization, supporting cohort members in their "investment in collaborative action," and encouraging the outcome of using personal and group empowerment to effect social change (Carr, 2003, p. 18). In addition to their roles as program ambassadors, cohort members develop personal mission statements incorporating tenets of socially responsible leadership and acknowledging their own assets for social change work. The next section discusses engaging cohort members in developing and delivering a campuswide event to reinforce that action.

Finally, an outcome embedded across learning activities is exhibiting a healthy self-concept. Research shows that aligning leadership efficacy (an internal belief in one's ability, actions, and ideas) and leadership capacity (possessing knowledge, skills, and attributes) helps individuals harness skills and resources in new, challenging, or complex situations, which is "especially relevant for students of color attempting to navigate institutional and societal structures designed to systematically privilege and oppress" (Dugan et al., 2012, p. 175). As a result of their participation and a by-product of their growing or sustained sense of empowerment, cohort members should report agility in pursuing personal, academic, and professional goals and an increased willingness to attain and use resources to further those goals. These learning outcomes are achieved to various degrees by each cohort member, but they are guided and encouraged through consistent participation in the program's various components.

Program Components

The WE program's components include bimonthly meetings; *anthropological excursions*, which is a borrowed term, defined here to mean group outings to apply lessons learned to real-world settings; joint and cross-program events; annual traditions; and Reaching for Academic Progress sessions, an early warning intervention that monitors academic progress.

Bimonthly workshops. Regular, twice-monthly events are the program's cornerstone and primarily consist of workshops with diverse speakers on topics with an analysis that celebrates the experiences and perspectives of women of color and supports their leadership development. Developed in concert with student affairs practitioners from across units and other experts in their fields, program managers support presenters in content development, homing in on research and practices and customizing workshops that specifically relate to the needs of women of color. It is important to note that the curriculum is linear in some respects; earlier workshops seek to arrive at a shared, if ever evolving, understanding of intersectionality, with later workshops focused on actualization.

Limited research separates women of color from the larger population of people of color or, frankly, from each other. While this makes it challenging to develop focused workshop content, it is also a compelling reason to do so. Consider it a contribution to the canon. Planning early, soliciting workshop presenters in advance, and knowing that participants will contribute to each topic as the experts of their experience will help overcome this challenge. By design, program staff are present during the workshops to support continuity between the events, help facilitate students' meaning making, and get an intimate perspective of participants' readiness and engagement so they can coach them through the process—all best practices for successful cocurricular program development. Similarly, the workshop development process includes best practices. The following are guidelines for workshop presenters:

- The structure should emphasize a balance of content sharing and interactivity.
- Content should demonstrate a sensitivity to systemic challenges associated with personal, professional, and leadership development for women of color and highlight positive and practical application now and in the future.

- Presenters should adhere to the belief that the workshop is a shared undertaking with cohort members, intentionally creating space for students to share individual experiences and their perspective of their community and culture of origin.

An institution's many departments present a valuable source of talent that can contribute to shaping and delivering this program component. At my institution, staff from the athletic and housing departments welcomed an opportunity to collaborate as a part of their effort to expand their reach, increase the diversity of their students, and incorporate innovative techniques in the delivery of their programs or services by literally meeting students where they are—a safe space that "encourage[s] them to explore more of their whole selves, which is critical given their daily negotiation of intersectionality" (Linder & Rodriguez, 2012, p. 393). Once a set of workshop offerings is developed, they can be updated and again offered to subsequent cohorts: the one-year participation model pays off in future dividends.

The associate director of my institution's financial fitness program presented a customized workshop titled Money Matters: Women of Color and Financial Fitness to support the program's mission of providing resources and tools to help students manage costs from freshman year through graduation and beyond. This workshop supports the outcome of demonstrating effective decision making related to personal financial management, incorporating research on the gender- and race-based wage gap, and the often overlooked and underdiscussed cultural practice of sending money home (Evans, 2006). It also emphasized proactive financial management and wealth attainment. With identities whose confluence may result in varying economic challenges, it's important for women of color college students to design financial plans that value and outline immediate steps toward financial independence and proficiency.

Another event of note is Why "WE" Rock, which was designed and delivered by cohort members with support from the program staff. During the spring, participants spend a portion of the bimonthly meetings dividing into committees, identifying chairwomen, and completing tasks outside meetings to offer a campuswide event designed to increase the visibility and recognition of women of color in the community. Charged with working collaboratively for a collective goal, cohort members delivered this program on March 1, designated as Women of Color Day by the National Institute for Women of Color, whose goals includes building a strong national network for women of African, Alaskan Native, American Indian, Asian, Hispanic, Latina, and Pacific Island heritages. Cohort members constructed a display in the student union and asked attendees and passersby to honor the women of color in their own lives, in and beyond the campus community, through dialogue, music, food, a preselected photo display, and a postcard collage cocreated by the community members. It was amazing to see nearly 90 attendees from various identity categories contribute to the collage, with one postcard reading,

> I am continually inspired by the amazing, strong, and resilient women of color [with whom] I organize, learn from, and spend time. I stand in awe of women of color feminists like Audre Lorde, bell hooks, Gloria Anzaldua, and Barbara Smith. I am indebted to their words.

Event attendees embraced the exciting challenge of acknowledging women of color as a necessary step to support their leadership trajectory, which is vital if we are to create a campus community in which all women of color are invested in the success of every member of the WE community.

Joint programming. A poignant early lesson for the WE program was engaging partners in its goals and delivery to ensure that students feel they matter to the campus community, when otherwise they may "feel marginalized more often than they feel that they matter, . . . which affects their self-concept and academic and social experiences on [and beyond] campus" (Jackson, 1998, p. 359). It is no small feat to have nearly doubled the number of events offered to cohort members during the program's second year, and it would have been impossible without collaborations and the inclusion of campuswide programs and events into the programming calendar.

Many campus partners offered formal opportunities for cohort members to participate in existing campus- and community-wide programs. When possible, these events were built into the WE program calendar alongside WE-specific events or offered as optional opportunities to explore elements of intersectionality. Our women's center was particularly generous in its support of the program, exemplifying partners' efforts to uniquely include the cohort, which ranged from reserving seats for the event to reserving roles for cohort members on the event planning board.

A program goal should also include expanding the support and recognition of women of color beyond the institution. Program managers from our institution and another local one collaborated during the program planning stage, identifying opportunities for participants to attend at least one large-scale event on each campus and extending invitations to other open events and social excursions. Participants then traveled together to events held on each other's campuses, gaining important and extended perspectives from other young women who were at the same stage and age of life and at institutions with different cultures, values, and norms. The most significant partnership, though, was with any brother program—in this case, the Men of Color Initiative, mentioned at the beginning of the chapter.

The value of participating across identity-conscious leadership development programs cannot be underscored enough. The programs are intended to serve students differently, as they have distinct goals and take varied approaches to realizing the departmental and divisional learning outcomes. There is something to be said, though, for engaging one another on issues that individually and collectively have an impact on those in communities of color in and beyond higher education. Joint offerings range from the workshop Shades of Proud, offered during lesbian, gay, bisexual, transgender, and questioning month to explore an additional dimension of intersectionality in communities of color, to Sex in the Dark, a workshop challenging perceptions about gender roles. With its tantalizing, double entendre title, Sex in the Dark offers a unique approach to dialogue, with attendees from both WE and the Men of Color Initiative seated in their same-gender huddles confidentially asking questions of participants in the other program. Eventually these conversations symbolically come into the light, with attendees physically coming together for discourse in full view of one another. As alluded to in the previous discussion of the campuswide event, these conversations and practices can and should additionally involve the entire campus community and certainly those groups collectively linked by a common history and daily realities. Gender and racial equity cannot be achieved in isolation, and research exploring authentic intersectional work teach us that examining identities, shared and distinct, is a "requirement for challenging the status quo" (Jennrich & Kowalski-Braun, 2014, p. 203).

Anthropological excursions. In addition to workshops co-led by program staff members, programmatic efforts include joint anthropological excursions. Designed to translate leadership lessons to a real-world application, an important program component includes excursions with an emphasis on social, cultural, and service-learning. Program staff solicit input from students, identify events at the college, and scour local events to find entertaining and informative excursions that draw connections to race, ethnicity, or gender, providing opportunities for cohort members to bond and, when relevant, commit to serving others. Many of the excursions were organic, time specific, and represented a unique part of each cohort's experience. As the cost of the excursions is generally covered for cohort members, this program component is also a contributing factor to employing a cohort model. In its second year of existence, the WE program's student staff led many of the social components, including optional campus partner events, anthropological excursions, and informal social activities, taking great care to help build cohort identity and program affinity.

WE and Men of Color offered an open workshop, Race, Gender, and Sports, co-led by each group's program managers and an assistant director from our athletics department, a former Division I athlete, to illustrate how deeply embedded stereotypes reveal themselves in college athletics. I mention this workshop in a discussion about excursions as an example of coupling workshops with an entertaining excursion, in this case a baseball game. By requiring excursion participants to attend the workshop, the programs achieved mutual goals of exposing attendees to the realities of intersectionality and planting a seed to view the related excursion with an intersectional lens.

An excursion that targets learning outcomes related to socially responsible leadership is the college's annual service day, which many institutions have established at the beginning of each academic year. Working in concert with members of the university ministry, which manages the program, and the alumni relations department to identify women of color alumnae and other supportive volunteers, program managers select relevant service sites, including a 5K run dedicated to advancing research on ovarian cancer that presents an opportunity for cohort members to locate their personal and leadership identities in the context of service and social responsibility.

Traditions. The use of rites of passage as a tool for college student development and retention predates identity-conscious programs. This cultural practice of creating, naming, and honoring traditions should be embedded into a successful WOCLP as time markers in the year-long experience. WE is marked by the Annual Retreat at the onset of the program and the Cohort Transition Brunch at its end. The retreat is an opportunity for the cohort members to build community through team building, set community standards, and review and affirm their commitment for the academic term. Subsequently, the end-of-year brunch, held during the program joining season, presents an opportunity for fellowship, reflection, and orientation for new cohort members. Outgoing cohort members share their experience and recommendations for the incoming cohort, students are noted for their contributions, and all receive a useful keepsake for their participation, which has included journals for reflection. Coffee, Cake, and Conversation, which is open to the women of color community at large and explicitly focuses on career success, is another time marker that is also a fundamental activity for WE participants.

The WE program does not dictate focused career exploration; rather, it emphasizes career success strategies that are particularly salient to women of color. While taking on various formats, the event consistently includes a cohort member speaking on the event's annual theme, welcomes professional women from the community to discuss their leadership and career paths, and provides an opportunity for women in the program and beyond to explore their curiosity and any concerns related to navigating the professional landscape for women of color. It equips students with tools and strategies to navigate possible barriers to bolster their potential for postcollege and career success. This is significant for women and women of color, as the real-world environment of the workplace offers continued and renewed challenges for balancing one's inside and outside identities. Leadership development, while deeply personal, must have a context, and many students rightly connect leadership skills to their future careers. In a study of similar leadership development programs for professional women, Ely, Ibarra, and Kolb (2011) noted that "establishing a safe space for learning and experimentation and building a community of peer support are critical elements of any effective leadership development program," with program participants "construct[ing] coherent and actionable narratives about who they are and wish to become [as professionals], grounded in candid assessments of the cultural, organizational and individual factors shaping them" (p. 487). While their article discusses leadership development programs for professional women, it represents an important philosophy that guides and is replicated at the large-scale event, focusing attention on career success for women of color.

Finally, cohort members received academic support through the department's early intervention process. The department monitors all program participants at each midterm period and participates in the college's academic early warning system. Participation in the process is voluntary, so to further build affinity and increase the likelihood that students will respond, the WE program manager is personally responsible for contacting cohort members with a midterm grade of a C- and below and scheduling one-on-one academic and personal success meetings with them. Comparatively speaking, cohort members represented a small number of all department participants whose grades warranted an intervention but garnered a 79% response rate for one-on-one meetings. It's important to note that although not a requirement, the entering cohort has consistently had a high grade point average (GPA). This defines a conundrum that may often be at the center of resistance for leadership development programming for women of color: They might not exhibit risk in the ways that colleges and universities tend to use to assess risk. In elevating and equalizing new measures of student success, such as resiliency and self-efficacy, with traditional measures of student retention, such as the cumulative GPA, the benefit of identity-conscious leadership development for women of color in higher education is undeniable.

Assessment: How Do You Know It Works?

Success for identity-conscious leadership programs for women of color college students is multifaceted as it includes success outcomes, such as improvements in leadership skills and knowledge and enhanced inter- and intrapersonal development and traditional measures of student retention, such as the cumulative GPA, year-to-year persistence rate, and graduation rates. Close attention should be paid to both types of measures to ensure a holistic assessment of participants' progress toward personal, social, and academic success. Real-time evaluations of program components allow participants to report the degree to which program goals are met, namely, through discrete inventories and tools to determine the efficacy of the workshop or activity; rate if the topics or experiences are relevant to the needs and concerns of women of color; and report how well workshops support open, honest, and respectful dialogue. These data are used to refine the topics offered on the program calendar and identify workshop leaders who are best equipped to support and enhance the leadership capacity of program participants. To assess intended learning outcomes, the WE program introduced a pre- and posttest centered on topics related to developing success skills.

Adapted from the Personal Progress Scale-Revised (PPS-R) and borrowed from the field of social work, the pre- and posttest measure the psychological and personal empowerment in women based on an increase of positive attitudes and behaviors associated with well-being (Johnson, Worell, & Chandler, 2005). The use of the PPS-R was modified to ask questions mapped against learning outcomes and measured participants' self-reported progress toward empowerment as a result of their program involvement. Results indicated that participants achieved overall growth, with cohort members reporting an improvement on 76% of the identified factors and positive maintenance on an additional 12% of identified factors related to empowerment. Use of the PPS-R in this setting is promising but limited; development as data is self-reported and captured at one point in time, which poses a challenge for a process that is ever evolving and whose outcomes may be tied to a number of variables. More research is needed for its wider implications for WOCLPs. While this model has been employed to great effect in a program serving women of color that endows participants with tools for performance at their highest capacity, opportunities remain for practitioners who intend to undertake creation and delivery of similar programs to expand and refine assessment of those efforts.

An important but uncharted opportunity for exploration is examining how participants apply learned skills and how a positive self-concept affects their leadership abilities and actions in other programs on campus and beyond. Additionally, reflection was a significant element of the program curriculum, and developing strategies to assess deeper learning that may occur during the reflective experience may be worthwhile. We also used an advisory board, whose role includes reviewing the program curriculum, including its assessment efforts, to obtain strategic advice about the program's content and delivery. While the board was underused because of time and resource constraints, the importance of meaningfully making use of broader campus efforts and partners is an important assessment goal. The reality is that program development and assessment for WOCLPs will continue to evolve. Success for such programs and for our students is not a goal but a journey. Taking part in that journey made the voices and experiences of WE participants real and can do so for all women of color whose unique experiences require an awareness, acknowledgment, and exploration of the independent and cumulative effects of their identities.

Conclusion

The story that opens this chapter, with its focus on resilience, renewal, and positive action, shows that inaction can no longer be an appropriate answer to the real and pervasive issue of meeting the needs of an increasingly diverse student body. Leadership development for women of color should help participants implement empowerment strategies to "strengthen [their] ongoing capacity for successful action under changing circumstances" (Carr, 2003, p. 11) and help students use that capacity in pursuit of personal, academic, and professional success.

Supporting women of color is not a zero-sum game, as there is no shortage of opportunities to take targeted approaches to address the needs of those with higher risk factors in higher education. As the opening story illustrates, acknowledging that we are all bound up together can in fact be a unifying and healing force. These women are, and have been, among us. They sit in our classrooms, live in our residence halls, and have the same aspirations and hopes for the future as their peers. I suggest forging a new paradigm by offering a program curriculum that provides a real opportunity to begin the process of closing the gap between the promises of higher education for women of color and the curriculum necessary to prepare them for the world beyond.

Action Items

- Assess the needs of women of color in your community. It is especially important for student affairs professionals to understand their institution's unique educational climate and to design a program relevant to these factors.

- Pay close attention to students' academic and social care. Helping students to be architects of their own development, even as they inelegantly as well as artfully negotiate the complexity of identity and leadership development, is an ongoing, challenging, and important process.
- Create an institutional imperative by involving institutional and area partners. Collaboration with other departments, programs, and student organizations helps expand the support and recognition of college women of color.

References

Carr, E. S. (2003). Rethinking empowerment theory using a feminist lens: The importance of process. *Affilia, 18*(1), 8–20.

Dugan, J. P., Kodoma, C. M., & Gebhardt, M. C. (2012). Race and leadership development among college students: The additive value of collective racial esteem. *Journal of Diversity in Higher Education, 5*(3), 174–189.

Ely, R. J., Ibarra, H., & Kolb, D. (2011). Taking gender into account: Theory and design for women's leadership development programs. *Academy of Management Learning & Education, 10*(3), 474–493.

Evans, C. E. (2006). *The intersection of gender, race, and culture as influencers on African American women's financial fitness, asset accumulation, and wealth attainment.* Retrieved from www.cew.umich.edu/research/pubs/econlaborpubs

Hur, M. H. (2006). Empowerment in terms of theoretical perspectives: Exploring a typology of the process and components across disciplines. *Journal of Community Psychology, 34*(5), 523–540.

Jackson, L. R. (1998). The influence of both race and gender on the experiences of African American college women. *Review of Higher Education, 21*(4), 359–375.

Jennrich, J., & Kowalski-Braun, M. (2014). "My head is spinning": Doing authentic intersectional work in identity centers. *Journal of Progressive Policy & Practice, 2*(3), 199–212.

Johnson, D. M., Worell, J., & Chandler, R. K. (2005). Assessing psychological health and empowerment in women: The Personal Progress Scale-Revised. *Women Health, 41*(1), 109–129.

Jones, S. R., & McEwen, M. K. (2000). A conceptual model of multiple dimensions of identity. *Journal of College Student Development, 41*(4), 405–414.

Kezar, A., & Moriarty, D. (2000). Expanding our understanding of student leadership development: A study exploring gender and ethnic identity. *Journal of College Student Development, 41*(1), 55–69.

Kodama, C., & Dugan, J. P. (2013). Leveraging leadership efficacy in college students: Disaggregating data to examine unique predictors by race. *Equity & Excellence in Education, 46*(2), 184–201.

Komives, S. R., Owen, J. E., Longerbeam, S. D., Mainella, F. C., & Osteen, L. (2005). Developing a leadership identity: A grounded theory. *Journal of College Student Development, 46*(6), 593–611.

Linder, C., & Rodriguez, K. L. (2012). Learning from the experiences of self-identified women of color activists. *Journal of College Student Development, 53*(3), 383–398.

Martínez Alemán, A. M. (2000). Race talks: Undergraduate women of color and female friendships. *Review of Higher Education, 23*(2), 133–152.

Nguyen, T. (Ed.). (2009). *"Language is a place of struggle": Great quotes by people of color*. Boston, MA: Beacon Press.

Opportunity gap. (2013). In *Glossary of Education Reform*. Retrieved from edglossary.org/opportunity-gap

Owen, J. E., Komives, S. R., Lucas, N., & McMahon, T. R. (Eds.). (2007). *Instructor's guide for exploring leadership: For college students who want to make a difference* (2nd ed.). San Francisco, CA: Jossey-Bass.

Renn, K. A., & Ozaki, C. C. (2010). Psychosocial and leadership identities among leaders of identity-based campus organizations. *Journal of Diversity in Higher Education, 3*(1), 14–26.

Shields, S. A. (2008). Gender: An intersectionality perspective. *Sex Roles: A Journal of Research, 59*(5), 301–311.

Sinclair-Chapman, V., Eloi, S., & King, S. (2014). The women of color circle: Creating, claiming and transforming spaces for women of color on a college campus. In D. Mitchell Jr., C. Y. Simmons, & L. A. Greyeribehl (Eds.), *Intersectionality in higher education* (pp. 219–228). New York, NY: Peter Lang.

Vasquez, M., & Comas-Díaz, L. (2007). Feminist leadership among Latinas. In J. L. Chin, B. Lott, J. K. Rice, & J. Sanchez-Hucles (Eds.), *Women and Leadership: Transforming Visions and Diverse Voices* (pp. 264–280). Oxford, UK: Blackwell.

White House Council on Women and Girls. (2014). *Women and girls of color: Addressing challenges and expanding opportunity*. Retrieved from www.whitehouse.gov/sites/default/files/docs/cwg_women_and_girls_of_color_report_112014.pdf

5

SOCIAL CAPITAL

Identity-Conscious Leadership Development Curricula for Students of Color

Jeff Brown and Nydia María Stewart

Ashley was a senior majoring in psychology, and she had performed academically well at a private, urban university in the Midwest. She was a first-generation college student and well on her way to being the first in her family to earn a college degree. She had on-campus and off-campus jobs but had managed to maintain a 3.3 grade point average. Ashley had been a dedicated member of the program she received her scholarship from when she was a senior in high school because of her commitment to working in underserved communities. Before college, Ashley managed to accumulate more than 200 hours of community service, which translated to an even greater zeal for service in college. To most people, Ashley was doing everything right. She had garnered a high level of respect from faculty and staff and was the envy of all her friends from her neighborhood. She had a great future ahead of her, but with 11 academic quarters under her belt, she began to experience feelings of emptiness and little to no sense of accomplishment. In all that Ashley had overcome and experienced in college, she still felt ill equipped to enter the real world of adulthood, filled with complex decisions and responsibilities.

Ashley had developed a strong relationship with her scholarship coordinator, Jeff Brown, and decided to set up a meeting to speak with him about the feelings she had been having. After a nearly hour-long conversation, Ashley had an epiphany that was confirmed and validated by her adviser. They had discovered a few things that with some coaching could change Ashley's life. In all that Ashley had done in college, she realized that she had not quite had a full college experience. She had worked hard academically, dedicated her extra time to working her two part-time jobs, and any time she had left was absorbed by her dedication to serving others. In the midst of a hectic schedule, Ashley never had time to really participate in any campus programs or student organizations. She had managed to complete her college career but let all the internship and study abroad opportunities pass her by. Ashley had only made time for school work and for maintaining the rigorous engagement requirements of her scholarship program. Her bachelor's degree was on the verge of conferral, but she had not quite developed, especially as a leader.

After much reflection, Ashley and her adviser realized that she actually missed out on the very thing she needed to be ready for life after graduation, but there was still an opportunity for her to participate in the leadership experiences she desired: her scholarship program.

Overview

Each summer, our scholarship coordinating team meets to conduct the program planning for the upcoming academic year. The summer after Jeff Brown met with Ashley, he decided that the planning process would have to address this key question of leadership development for all the scholars supported by his department. We had just completed a year during which we managed a suite of scholarships for more than 35 first-generation, low-income students of color who participated in four different scholarship programs that awarded from $10,000 to $16,500 per year. All the funds allocated to students came from well-intentioned donors who wanted to help underserved students achieve their dream of going to college and getting a good education. In return, these students were expected to give a little of their time by serving others through community service work and adhering to a few basic scholarship requirements. At the time, the scholarship coordinator had spent seven years working to make innovations and to enhance the student experience while attending to the unique needs of the suite of scholarships he was tasked to oversee. During that time, the programmatic curriculum focused on two core areas: academic excellence and community service.

After the encounter with Ashley, we realized the scholarship curriculum had to expand beyond these foundational learning outcomes and contract requirements. The key questions we wrestled with were, What can we do to enhance the experience for these scholars so they can be more successful during their time in college and after they receive their degrees? If we have four or five years of time with student scholars, how can we build a progressive curriculum to empower them to have an optimal university experience? These questions were critical to the development of our curriculum and, more important, to the successful development of our scholars' leadership capacities.

After a discussion and brainstorming session, we realized that an informal curriculum had existed in the program for a number of years, hidden in the way we were advising students to take advantage of the rest of the university. When we met with the scholars, we were always challenging them to connect across campus and acquire the tools and experiences that could propel them to success. We referred them to many other programs, departments, and resources to make sure they developed a network of support to help with their most complex needs. We monitored their academic progress and communicated with their professors to make sure they stayed on track. We exposed them to social justice concepts, service immersion projects, and a myriad of other opportunities, all in the name of developing the whole student. But after evaluating all the things to which we attempted to expose these students, the one thing missing from the equation was development in the area of leadership. The experiences that most closely resembled leadership skill building were perhaps being addressed in unofficial ways, but we could not say with great certainty that our scholars were really developing as leaders. In addition, we noticed clear developmental gaps in scholars like Ashley from our extensive interactions with them. We felt that a comprehensive leadership curriculum would lead to a better, more engaging experience and result in increased transformative learning, higher levels of retention, and more timely graduation for the scholars.

The retention, persistence, and graduation rates for low-income students of color continue to be a matter of great concern for public and private institutions alike. Colleges and universities expend countless resources to address this sometimes overwhelming problem of retaining students on the margins and addressing their unique needs. The life skills and other capacities students develop on the path to graduation should be of equal concern to higher education institutions. In other words, what are students learning as they matriculate, and what will they be able to take with them after they graduate?

Institution administrators want students who have enrolled, attended classes, and paid good money in the process to not only graduate with diploma in hand but also become positive ambassadors for the school. They want students to take all they have learned and go out into the world and change it for the better. This can only happen when institutions invest time and resources in developing these students as leaders through cocurricular engagement, in addition to the learning that happens in the classroom.

Leadership development programs can be found across a wide range of colleges and universities, and students increasingly are demanding leadership certificate programs, cocurricular transcripts, and leadership e-portfolio tools that can assist them in transitioning to the world of work after completing their degrees. When we set out to develop an identity-conscious leadership curriculum specifically for low-income students of color, there were few to no resources to help us get started. After agreeing that this group of students needed attention in the area of leadership in a way that may be different from that of their privileged peers, we recognized that something new and innovative needed to be created.

Chapter Framework

As we developed a leadership curriculum designed to meet the unique needs of our scholars, we researched past models of leadership development and looked for ones that considered the students' social identities. An abundance of literature addresses the theme of race and leadership (Ospina & Foldy, 2009); unfortunately, this body of work was limiting because the literature seldom neatly intersected race and other social identities in the discussion of leadership development. The students in our scholarship programs were mostly students of color, but many also identified as low income or first generation, and we needed to remain mindful of this.

We also looked at leadership development as a tool for retention and persistence, which introduced another element that had to be considered. The goal then became to compile a number of leadership competencies that would combine cultural awareness, portable skills, and an understanding of the noncognitive variables that contributed to student success. If our students could obtain these skills, we knew we would create transformative learners who would persist, graduate, and develop as leaders.

Identity Consciousness

Upon assessing the needs of our target population, we developed a leadership curriculum intended to build social capital among some of our higher-risk students. This curriculum was designed with an identity-conscious framework, taking into consideration the importance of risk factors and students' individual racialized and socioeconomic experiences. With these identities in mind, we developed a workshop series with specific skill-set-focused outcomes. The workshops were also conducted in an intentional order, starting with the Leadership 101 workshop and ending with a capstone workshop on the social change model (Astin & Angeles, 1996). Each workshop had a set of learning outcomes to serve as an additional framework and to assist in assessment.

Assessment of this curriculum was an integral part of its success. It not only identified for our department and division the kind of learning that took place but also helped develop an expanded leadership curriculum for students. Through quantitative pre- and posttesting as well as qualitative workshop assessments, we were able to gauge students' self-efficacy and growth from the beginning of the curriculum to the end.

Curriculum Breakdown

Once we had an outline of themes and desired outcomes (see Table 5.1), the workshops were fairly easy to develop and were intended to be clear cut, developmental, and easy to digest for the students. As we considered our themes through an identity-conscious lens, it was clear that our students needed to be at the center of everything we did rather than just being the recipients of information.

Workshop 1: Leadership 101

The first workshop is centered on different kinds of leadership. For students of color, leadership tends to be centered on leadership positions rather than leadership experiences. Demystifying the leadership experience for our students was a necessary first step to get them to see themselves as leaders. The first workshop was designed to expose them to different kinds of leadership

TABLE 5.1
Workshop Themes and Outcomes

Workshop	*Desired Outcome*
Leadership 101	Introducing different models of leadership, encouraging student reflection on desired leadership styles
Identity development	Introducing social identities, systems of power, privilege, and oppression; encouraging student reflection on intersection of personal identities and leadership
Communication and code switching	Building and practicing verbal communication skills; identifying speech codes, code switching, and authenticity in professional voice
Managing group dynamics and conflict	Identifying individual conflict management style and roles in group settings
Self-efficacy	Defining self-efficacy and developing resilience and self-confidence
Social change model capstone	Applying all skills developed during workshop series and applying them to aspects of the social change model (Astin & Angeles, 1996)

to get them thinking about how they fit into different models and theories of leadership. At a mission-driven institution, we make sure to focus on ethics, social responsibility, and leadership for social change. These themes make leadership more accessible to higher-risk students of color because they emphasize the journey and qualities of leadership rather than a top-down model of leadership through power and position.

The leadership framework we used, socially responsible leadership, was developed by our university's student leadership institute. This framework of leadership is central to how our university as a whole develops leadership in our students. The five tenets of socially responsible leadership covered in this workshop are self-understanding and personal integrity, taking the perspective of others seriously, contributing to a larger community, knowledge and intellectual competence, and striving for excellence. These five tenets allowed us to engage in conversations with students about how they lead, even outside specific leadership positions, and how they see themselves evolving in their leadership.

Following the breakdown and definition of the five tenets, the students participated in an activity on ethical decision making in which the students were presented with different ethical dilemmas and were asked to use the tenets of socially responsible leadership to justify their decisions. We also reviewed several ethical decision-making pitfalls from the Josephson Institute of Ethics (2014), such as, "If no one gets hurt, it's okay" and "If it's necessary, it's ethical."

The workshop contained the following components:

- Introduction of socially responsible leadership
- Review of the five tenets
- Discussion of various ethical dilemmas in small groups
- Large-group discussion of the decision-making process and how socially responsible leadership relates to this process
- Discussion on the kind of leader each student would like to be

Workshop 2: Identity Development

Our identity development workshop was an important starting point for students before we took them into further specific skill development. As we developed this curriculum with an identity-conscious framework, it was important for the content delivery to mirror our theory. Through our partnership with our cultural programs office, we brought in an expert facilitator to conduct a workshop that provided students with insight into power, privilege, and systems of oppression that exist in society. Students participated in introspective exercises to identify their social identities and systems of power and privilege as well as how they interact with people who are different from them. The purpose of this workshop was to provide an identity foundation for the students to take with them as they navigated the remaining workshops. It was important for us to refer to this workshop and restate its importance when we delivered more specific social capital-building, skills-based content so our students could see that their identities are an important aspect of their leadership development.

The identity development workshop contained the following components:

- Story of your name: In this activity, students review the story of their name and how it affects their identity. Discussion follows.
- Identity saliency: Students review their social identities and how they have an impact on their everyday lives. Discussion follows on which identities are most important to them and why.
- Systems of power, privilege, and oppression: Review systems of power and privilege with the students. Define *privilege, power, oppression*, and other key terms to think about how identities interact on a systems level.
- Recap and process the workshop experience.

Workshop 3: Communication and Code Switching

This was the first workshop we envisioned when identifying skills necessary for building social capital in our students, and it was also the skill area our students were the most deficient in based on our assessment. (This workshop was conducted in two parts, although students later reported the two content areas could have been entire workshops on their own.) The first portion of the workshop was about communication and designed to address common pitfalls in public speaking. Because most college students must at some point give a presentation or speech, this workshop focused on addressing groups of 20 or more people. Students were asked to stand up and give a one-minute speech on how their previous quarter went. Although this may seem miniscule, it was an important opportunity to identify specific physical and speech patterns that are distracting to an audience. It was also necessary to discuss how nervousness manifests itself in the body and how to calm down to minimize the visible results.

The second portion of the workshop was about professional code switching. For the purposes of this workshop, *code switching* was defined as a change in speech pattern that is dependent on one's surroundings. The most important point to drive home in this workshop was that a student's *home code*, or the manner in which they naturally speak, is not better than or worse than their *professional code*, or the manner in which they speak in their desired profession. We were intentional in addressing this because of the anecdotal perception of code switching as assimilation or whitening of speech. Wheeler and Swords's (2001) model provided a great context for not assigning value to one form of speaking over another. Given that this curriculum is centered on identity consciousness, it is important not to invalidate the experiences of students who speak differently at home or in their communities. The skill-building portion focused on learning vernacular for a certain field, identifying a desirable pace, and removing colloquialisms from speech when possible. It is important to note that most students of color in our workshops knew what code switching is (even if not by name) and reported doing it for most of their lives. The skills we were teaching them were not brand new, but giving them the language for it helped empower them to feel competent in professional settings.

The communication and code switching workshop contained the following components:

- Public speaking tips and tricks: Students practice speaking to the group, reviewing common mishaps in public speaking, and how to work through nervousness.
- Code switching: Provide a definition and overview.
- Professionalism and authenticity discussion: What does the "professional you" sound like? How can one stay authentic in professional settings while code switching?

Workshop 4: Managing Group Dynamics and Conflict

This workshop was designed with the intent to get away from passive-aggressive and conflict-avoidant behaviors that can hurt group dynamics. Students report often experiencing conflict, especially in group project settings. However, they also overwhelmingly report doing whatever is necessary to avoid the conflict altogether. In this workshop, students participated in different personality assessments to help them develop a deeper understanding of how they function and what they can do to be their best selves alone and in groups. It is important to note that there is no magic assessment for students to understand themselves, and practitioners can use whichever assessment works for them or their institution. It is most important to use an assessment that honors and identifies personality types that are nondominant. When delivering an identity-conscious leadership curriculum, it can be difficult to find an assessment that rings true for students of color or low-income students. If this is the case, it is important to address this fact in the workshop and let the students talk about it. This way, they can more easily segue into how their personality types and working styles surface in conflict. Assessments that can be used to frame these conversations are the Meyers-Briggs Type Indicator, StrengthsQuest, True Colors, and Emergenetics, among others.

The conflict portion of this workshop is another key element and intentional point of this curriculum. Low-income students, first-generation students, and students of color are often marginalized at institutions of higher education. This can inform how they experience conflict and work through it. They may feel disenfranchised in conflict and wish to disengage, or they may experience battle fatigue. Low-income, first-generation, and students of color are often ill equipped to navigate universities generally, and conflict can cause them to lose momentum in their studies and shut down.

For this portion of the workshop, students were placed in groups, given different scenarios of conflict, and instructed to come up with solutions as a group. Given different styles of conflict management based on their personality assessments, students were able to discuss with each other how their specific conflict management style informed the result they chose. To process this portion of the workshop, we discussed how participants' identities and the identity saliency exercises they completed in previous workshops might affect their personality type and conflict management style.

The group dynamics and conflict workshop contained the following components:

- Personality assessment and discussion: Group students by personality type and ask them to discuss how they see themselves in that type.
- Conflict resolution scenarios and discussion: How do students' personality types affect their conflict management styles? How do their identities affect their conflict management style?
- Debriefing session and closing discussion.

Workshop 5: Self-Efficacy

This workshop was important to include in this series because low-income students, first-generation students, and students of color often enter college with low levels of self-efficacy or low levels of belief in their own abilities. Through this workshop, students were able to identify their motivation for doing different activities and how they chose their major or career field. Self-efficacy, or their own belief in their abilities, was a big draw for students to enter a certain field. However, we did find, through conversations about life after college, that some students felt they were not adequately equipped to enter the workforce. This workshop allowed students to explore how confidence in their abilities informs their performance in certain realms. Another contributing factor to self-efficacy discussed in this workshop was the concept

of failure. Our highest risk students are most prone to considering one failure (on a test, quiz, or paper) as indicative of their entire skill set or ability.
Providing them with the space to discuss how they define failure and helping
them push through is important in developing their self-efficacy and resilience. The opportunity for students to identify their skill sets and develop
enough confidence in them to push through setbacks is an integral part of
leadership skill building for low-income students, first-generation students,
and students of color.

The self-efficacy workshop contained the following components:

Paper toss activity: Ask students to volunteer to throw balled-up paper
into a waste bin. Discuss who volunteered and why. For the students who
did not volunteer, discuss why not. In our experience we found that the
students who volunteered to perform this task in front of a group of their
peers did so because they either felt confident in their abilities or wanted
the challenge of trying. Students who did not volunteer expressed fear of
failure in front of their peers or a dislike for the activity in general. This
conversation was a natural segue into self-efficacy and confidence. The
following are possible discussion questions:

- How did you choose your major?
- Have you ever failed at something? How was that experience, and
  did you try again?
- What impact does your idea of your own ability have on how you
  choose your personal and professional pursuits
- Define *self-efficacy* for students: Discuss why identity matters in
  self-efficacy as well as goal setting, managing success and failure,
  and stress management. It is particularly important to discuss the
  high and low self-efficacy outcomes associated with each.
- Share stories: Talk about experiences with self-efficacy, goal setting,
  managing success and failure, and smanaging stress.

Workshop 6: Social Change Model Capstone

In this workshop, students were prompted to connect all the skills developed
in previous leadership workshops to their ability to act as change agents based
on the social change model (Astin & Angeles, 1996). Students were given the
opportunity to connect their increased skills and social capital to their ability to promote equity and social justice in their classrooms, communities,
and careers. We made this the capstone to the workshop series because an
additional purpose of this identity-conscious curriculum was to empower

students to go forth and actively participate in transformative processes connected to the greater good. With the skills they developed and concepts they were beginning to master, the students needed a workshop in which they were called to action rather than left with a variety of disparate reflections and no plan for how to apply what they learned to their life. This curriculum was not just about building social capital for our higher-risk students but also about helping mold them into leaders who can and will do the same for others.

Assessment: How Do You Know It Works?

To assess the success of the leadership curriculum, students were asked to fill out a pretest at the beginning of the academic year, individual surveys following each workshop, and a posttest and to participate in a focus group. The pretest was a self-evaluation of students' leadership skills and development using a Likert scale model. Through this pretest, we were able to compile quantitative data that would assist in the overall assessment and provide a better foundation for the qualitative portion of the assessment. The posttest contained the same questions to assess students' growth and development throughout the year. The individual workshop surveys qualitatively assessed what was learned from each workshop, along with the professional and personal applications of the skills learned. The major themes for each workshop were identified if at least two students mentioned that theme in their response.

Through this assessment we learned how students engage with the workshop material and how to improve content areas for further development. Student feedback indicated a need for various presentation styles; for example, students felt they would be better engaged through case studies, more small-group activities, and interactive workshops. Along with presentation style, students also gave feedback regarding the physical space for the workshops, indicating that a traditional classroom setting is not the most conducive to their participation. The following were topics suggested by students for future consideration: interviewing skills; mental, physical, and emotional health and how they can be applied to being a leader; and topics pertaining to specific majors. Assessment of this curriculum will continue to ensure a rich and developmental experience for all students.

Conclusion

The most important thing we came across in developing this curriculum was to stay true to its intended purpose: filling gaps in social capital and building capacity for the low-income students, first-generation students, and students of color in our scholarship programs. Holding true to this purpose is what made this program so successful. We tailored the curricular content to the needs we saw in our students. Creating a workshop series for the sake of generic development or exposure is not enough for our highest-risk students. We know that marginalized students succeed in the classroom when their academic curriculum engages their social identities, and we set out to design a leadership curriculum that did the same.

To make this work at your institution, you must look at the overall landscape of risk for your target students and allow this context to inform the skills and capacities you focus on. The curricular themes presented in this chapter are applicable to most low-income students, first-generation students, and students of color, but it is important to mold them in accordance with the nuances of your students. Code switching might look different at a predominantly White institution versus a historically Black college or university. Developing capacities for self-efficacy might be particularly difficult at an elite liberal arts college or at an institution focused on science, technology, engineering, and mathematics. These local contexts must be taken into consideration when incorporating this curriculum at your institution.

Just as taking note of your campus climate and landscape is key to developing relevant content, it is equally important to use the services already provided for students at your institution. We were purposeful in creating relationships with offices like financial fitness, the career center, and cultural programs to create a curriculum tailored to our students. Many institutions of higher education have all these services and more for students, but they often do not take the students' identities into consideration when delivering them. When we established partnerships with these offices, we were careful to let them know that we were not interested in duplicating services but rather in collaborating to make the workshop content specifically relevant for low-income students, first-generation students, and students of color.

A warning on how to manage these conversations at your institution: Do not approach campus partnerships from a deficit model. It is never wise to tell office personnel that they are underserving a specific student population. This is about building bridges, not burning them. When we were approaching offices to work with, it was first important to identify possible allies in those spaces. Were staff members taking their work in an identity-conscious direction? Knowing how to frame the conversation is important because it not advisable to simply bring in a staff member to do a presentation that does not use an identity-conscious framework. You want to make sure you are bringing in student affairs educators who can balance their expertise in a content area with knowledge about their audience.

The delivery style and pedagogy of an identity-conscious workshop series that builds social capital is just as important as the content. As you work through content with your partners, take note of their intended presentation style, use of language, and general sensitivity to higher-risk student populations. Remember to use your expertise in how to serve low-income students, first-generation students, and students of color when discussing methods for content presentation. Do your students respond well to classroom settings? Do you have the ability to deliver transformative content via a retreat or experiential learning opportunities? Do not be afraid to think creatively and gauge what works best for your students. This critical engagement with partners on the front end will yield incredible gains for your students in the long run.

Action Items

As you develop your identity-conscious leadership curriculum, the following specific steps can help make it successful:

- Gauge your campus climate and the unique needs of your students. If you are creating a curriculum for students you advise or supervise, this part will be easier than if you are creating a curriculum without a captive audience. Advising sessions and one-on-one meetings are perfect places to gather information from your students about their experiences with leadership on campus. Do they see themselves as leaders? How do they define *leadership*? Asking your students these questions directly may prove more effective than any campus climate survey. Once you have a good idea of the kind of leadership experiences your students have had, the next step is to identify other places on campus that offer leadership skill development.
- Identify campus partners and allies to assist in the delivery of content. A huge part of developing the content of our curriculum was about identifying partnerships rather than insourcing everything ourselves. We knew there were great student affairs educators on campus providing a variety of relevant workshops; they just may not have been tailored to our student population with an identity-conscious framework. Who are the key players doing leadership development on your campus? Set up a meeting with them to collaborate on how to best serve your students.
- Develop the curriculum's delivery style. An identity-conscious curriculum is about engaging students at the intersections of identity that shape their collegiate experience *and* employing a pedagogy that

is effective with the students you are working with. Do your students learn as much from each other as they learn from you? Do they thrive in group dialogue? Are they hands-on learners? Do they learn by doing? It is hoped that you know the answers to these questions for your students, but if you do not, you do not necessarily have to conduct a campuswide assessment before you begin your curriculum design process. You can gather this information quickly by asking the students you already serve key questions to inform your design process. Once you are running a pilot program, you can conduct a deeper assessment to inform innovations in your curriculum. Making this an identity-conscious endeavor means not only understanding students' developmental needs but also knowing how to deliver content in a way that will best resonate with them.

References

Astin, H., & Angeles, C. (1996). *A social change model of leadership development: Guidebook: Version III*. Los Angeles: Higher Education Research Institute, University of California, Los Angeles.

Josephson Institute of Ethics. (2014). *Making ethical decisions*. Retrieved from www.sfjohnson.com/acad/ethics/making_ethical_decisions.pdf

Ospina, S., & Foldy, E. (2009). A critical review of race and ethnicity in the leadership literature: Surfacing context, power and the collective dimensions of leadership. *Leadership Quarterly, 20*(6), 876–896.

Wheeler, R., & Swords, R. (2001, November). *"My goldfish name is Scaley" is what we say at home: Code-switching—a potent tool for reducing the achievement gap in linguistically diverse classrooms*. Paper presented at the annual meeting of the National Council of Teachers of English, Baltimore, MD.

6

CAREER DISCERNMENT AND CAREER CAPITAL DEVELOPMENT FOR STUDENTS OF COLOR AND FIRST-GENERATION COLLEGE STUDENTS

Richard P. Morales and Eric Mata

Jennifer was a successful student who was a few months from ending her undergraduate career. She excelled in leadership positions on campus, academics, and as a student worker in our office. Her success in and outside the classroom led to a full scholarship to graduate school in her field of interest. For most students, this situation was ideal, but for Jennifer it presented a difficult choice: attend graduate school and begin her professional career or stay in Chicago to be close to her family.

Jennifer, who identifies as Latina, was the first in her family to go to college, and, like most first-generation students of color, she had no access to professional relationships to help her make the transition to life after college. She had the opportunity to work in a psychology lab in another state under the tutelage of a faculty member whose work influenced Jennifer's career path, but she also felt the pull of her family's desire for her to stay in Chicago. Jennifer was challenged to find ways to engage her family in critical conversations about departure. She often felt as though she would not even be a good candidate for the job. She struggled through her search process because she had not spent a lot of time prior to her senior year thinking about what life after college might be like.

As with most retention programs, much of our work with first-generation students and students of color focuses on creating academic, social, and mentoring experiences to help them graduate from a four-year university. Many of our most active first-generation students and students of color took advantage of the services these programs offered; however, most were not prepared for what would happen after they crossed the stage at graduation.

To begin our work, we had to ask ourselves an important question: Why were students of color and first-generation students not prepared to achieve once they earned a degree?

Overview

Working with students of color and first-generation students at a large urban, private university, we found that many of our students were shocked by the real world as it related to their career development. Many of our first-generation students and students of color were not finding jobs within three months after graduation. Those who did find entry-level jobs after graduation often found positions that were not related to their majors; instead, they were in areas they were not passionate about. This led to many of our graduating students coming back to campus to talk about their career concerns and look for ways to connect their identity and values to their career aspirations. What was most troubling was that many of the students who were having these issues had been highly involved on campus in a variety of leadership positions and were a part of a strong mentoring program that has been shown to positively affect a student's ability to be successful. For our team, it raised three questions: First, what was missing in the student experience for first-generation students and students of color that left them ill prepared for career success? Second, if career success was low for our most highly engaged students, what was happening with students who were less engaged? Third, what can we do to increase career access for first-generation students and students of color while they are in college?

In higher education, retention programs are often created to assist students of color and first-generation students achieve academic success while enrolled in college. For example, many universities have established strong mentoring, academic tutoring, and diversity programming efforts to ensure that students of color and first-generation students have the tools and the safe space to succeed in college. However, as student affairs educators, we assume that students of color and first-generation students will have easier access to better career opportunities, postbaccalaureate educational opportunities, and higher socioeconomic class status once they graduate. Yet while working with these students, we are seeing a career exploration barrier during college and an achievement gap beyond college.

This chapter challenges student affairs educators to think differently about the intersection of identity and career discernment and engagement. We need to rethink how we develop a retention curriculum to include career-related interventions. The addition of a career-focused curriculum can increase retention by creating a more focused undergraduate experience for our students. Finally, we know that self-efficacy is a key driver for retention and can come from career engagement. Focusing on self-efficacy as a way to increase career capital is essential in moving students toward a more successful postcollege experience.

Chapter Framework

We know first-generation students and students of color face additional challenges when attending college. As with most university retention initiatives, academic and mentoring programs were created to increase college success, but these programs had little or no career preparation focus. When working with first-generation students and students of color, it is equally important to create career-related interventions that increase their career self-efficacy during college.

Many first-generation students and students of color struggle with family-related stresses in the context of career planning, which include pressure to support family members, misalignment of academic or career goals and family values, and anxiety from trying to gain approval from parents (Constantine & Flores, 2006). Constantine and Flores (2006) found that African American, Latina/Latino, and Asian American students exhibited more ambiguity about their career paths when they also experienced psychological distress over family concerns. Therefore, providing career-related interventions, such as personalized career coaching, addresses these identity-related issues by providing needed career information and a venue to express family-related stress.

When working with first-generation students and students of color on their career development, it is important to think about how to create intentional discernment experiences focused on how their personal experiences, values, and identity connect to their career plans. The sophomore year is a perfect opportunity to begin establishing a strong structure of career discernment experiences. In her qualitative study, Schaller (2005) interviewed 19 sophomore students to find what experiences these students were facing during their sophomore year. Schaller found they had three areas of frustration: personal reflection, reflection on their relationships, and their academic experience. In addition, students who engaged in structured deep reflection increased their understanding of how their values connected to their career interests. This increased their confidence in their career plans; that is, they were less frustrated and had a clearer view of their academic or professional path. As a result, students felt more empowered to plan for their future by applying for jobs and talking with their professors about graduate school options before their junior year (Schaller, 2005).

For first-generation students and students of color to achieve postcollege success, career-relevant interventions should focus on enhancing their career capital. The idea of career capital is derived from the lack of a social network for postcollege actions such as choosing a graduate program, seeking profession-related information, or exploring postgraduate options after college (Rios Agular & Deil-Amen, 2012). Career capital consists of (a) building relationships with people in a career the students are seeking, (b) gaining access to information and resources about their career interests, and (c) participating in career exposure experiences related to their career choice. Providing first-generation students and students of color structured career capital development experiences not only increases their knowledge of career-related resources but also improves their career self-efficacy.

To truly assist first-generation students and students of color to achieve postcollege success, staff must involve themselves in research and in conversations about how identity and personal and family experiences affect students' career choices and then use that information to create learning experiences from the ground up. To do this, we must keep in mind that structured discernment experiences matter. Many of these students are working to support themselves or their families' needs. This does not leave much time for them to engage in meaningful discernment experiences about their career plans. Finally, first-generation students and students of color need access to career capital experiences to ensure their postcollege success. This is extremely important as many first-generation students and students of color do not have access to personal networks and experiences related to their career plans to increase their career exposure, knowledge, and career self-efficacy.

Identity Consciousness

In reflecting on our own experiences as student affairs professionals, one of the things we came to understand was that both of us were first-generation college students. Additionally, we realized that our status as white-collar professionals meant that our identities as first-generation students have evolved

and stayed with us as we made the transition from college student to graduate student and now as professionals.

With further reflection, we came to understand that in each iteration of
our identities as first-generation, we went through the same type of experiences that often inhibited us or created roadblocks to sustained success. In
the same way that first-generation college students experience college differently than their peers, first-generation graduate students experience graduate school differently than their peers. An important part of the reflection
experiences we have created for our students is to help them understand the
unique skills they have developed through their success as first-generation
undergraduate students and how these unique skills can help them as they
move into the next chapter as either first-generation graduate students or
first-generation white-collar professionals.

By taking an identity-conscious approach to career development, we are
able to help students discern the ways their identities might affect their major
and career choices. For example, we might begin to explore why a female
student who excels at math might shy away from a career in accounting. We
might also begin to explore why some of our male students who enjoy volun-
teering with young people might not be pulled toward a career in education.
But more important, an identity-conscious approach allows us to create a
deeper and more meaningful understanding of the ways the social constructs
of race, gender, socioeconomic status, and first-generation status might affect
students on a systemic level. This understanding can then allow us to create
more structured interventions, such as the following.

Career choke point. To address some of the concerns brought up in the
introduction to this chapter, we began to ask when, during a student's four-
year experience, could we make the most impact on his or her career success? Based on the research, we decided that the sophomore year made the
most sense. Traditionally, most college students wait until their senior year
to begin thinking about what they want to do for a career, leading students
to rush their career search and make choices about their career path that
lack a necessary level of critical thinking and discernment. However, first-
generation and students of color faced additional barriers to their ability to
be better prepared for career success after graduation. These barriers end up
creating what is referred to as a *career choke point.*

The career choke point occurs in students experiencing the sophomore slump, characterized by increased academic stress, a lack of personal
awareness, and a decreased sense of community. When working with first-
generation students and students of color, we discovered that in addition to
the typical challenges of the sophomore slump, these students experienced
a lack of personal reflection and minimal engagement in career exploration

experiences. Many of these students were the first in their family to attend college, and while this was a personal success for them and their families, we saw increased anxiety and confusion during their sophomore year because of a lack of social capital in their personal networks (parents, siblings, and friends) to prepare for career success after graduation. As a result, first-generation students and students of color experience a choke point that either leads to attrition after their sophomore year or to moving through college unclear about their major and career choice.

Career capital. The personal networks of people, resources, and information used to gain access to information that will inform a college student's career choice before graduation are called *career capital.* When working with first-generation students and students of color to increase their career success, we found that many of these students did not have access to the career capital they needed to make an informed career choice before graduation. Furthermore, they did not know how to gain career capital while in college. Many of them had to work to support themselves through college and played significant roles in their families, thus limiting their opportunity to engage in career discernment and capital-building experiences on their own.

As with most universities, these students had access to a career center on campus; however, they rarely used the resources it offered. This lack of use resulted in limited structured mentoring, resources, and information as well as low career self-efficacy in students' ability to think about their professional options early in their college career. This resulted in students delaying their career plans until late in their senior year, which often led to uninformed career choices after graduation.

In the next section we offer tangible, career-related interventions to help first-generation students and students of color achieve postcollege success, including one-on-one and group experiences that address four specific phases that occur during students' sophomore to senior years. For each phase, a program or one-on-one experience is provided to address the specific career-related learning outcome for that phase using an identity-conscious approach.

Building a Career-Intervention Road Map

To turn what we found while working with first-generation students and students of color into a program that was intentional and driven by outcomes, we knew we had to create a multiyear program that addressed the findings we discovered. We divided this program into the following four distinct phases that began with the sophomore year and ended with the first postgraduation year: discernment, action, preparation, and capturing success. Each phase is designed to build students' career capital.

Discernment: The Sophomore Experience

We know that students who experience what Schaller (2005) refers to as the sophomore slump are often not engaged in critical reflection on their values and how they connect to their career plans. We also know that first-generation college students are often less likely to practice this type of reflection or discernment than students whose parents are able to provide them with the necessary information to make progress toward a possible career. Therefore, the idea behind the sophomore experience, discernment, was to create structured involvement opportunities by implementing a career coaching model that would allow students to engage in the reflection necessary for them to avoid the sophomore slump. The basic premise of the career coaching model is to move students toward the creation of a tangible, goals-driven career plan. Another end goal of the sophomore experience is to prepare students to best use the career center on campus, which was important because we were meeting with students who were not fully taking advantage of the services offered by the career center. Additionally, through our partnership with the career center, we were able to determine that first-generation students and students of color were in fact underusing their services.

The year-long curriculum is designed to cover three topics: building career capital and access; connecting major, values, and career options; and financial fitness and quality of life. Through the career coaching process, students are invited to meet with their career coach for a 30- to 40-minute meeting at least once a quarter. Figure 6.1 provides an example of the format of an initial meeting with a student. One of the more important action items we encourage participants to commit to is the creation of an online portfolio. We walk them through the process of creating a portfolio and explain why it is important to have one in an increasingly creative marketplace. We then focus on the creation process, which includes gathering information to include in the portfolio, selecting a platform for hosting it, creating the portfolio, reviewing the portfolio, and seeking feedback and updating it as necessary. First-generation students of color struggled with their career self-efficacy, but the online portfolios allowed these students to promote their personal brand to help build their career-self efficacy when choosing a career and gave them confidence to pursue their intended major by allowing them to highlight the work they have already done through courses, leadership experiences, and so on.

By the end of the career coaching curriculum and the creation of their online portfolio, students will have developed a tangible, step-by-step action plan they can follow as they move into their junior year.

Self-assessment is an important component of the career coaching curriculum. We work diligently with students to help them develop critical

Figure 6.1 Meeting 1: Building career capital and access.

Outcomes:

- Explain the meaning of career capital.
- Reflect on students' career plans, where they are in those plans, and whether they have built enough career capital.
- Outline an action plan to access staff and resources pertaining to students' career plans.

1. Purpose and overview of career coaching: Explain to students the purpose of career coaching and why we track their progress.
2. Reflect on ideal career plans: Ask students what their ideal career or graduate school plans are.
3. Define *career capital.*
4. Dialogue: Discuss building career capital and accessing DePaul career resources.
   a. Share your story: A staff member shares stories about his or her own career journey and the importance of building career capital to learn information about students' career of choices.
   b. Identify career exploration activities (CEA): Help students identify one to two CEAs they can complete. Review the CEA database or calendar for a list of CEAs.
   c. Access people: If students have access to people or professional mentors to assist them with their career exploration, help them list questions for an informational meeting. If they don't have access to people to talk with about their careers, have them research mentors in the alumni network.
   d. Get familiar with the career center: Familiarize students with the career center.
   e. Discuss the university job board: Make sure students are aware of its importance and send them to its website to review internships they might be interested in.
   f. Explain O*NET Online: Send them a link (www.onetonline.org) to this resource that provides information on occupations.
   g. Share other online tools:
      1. Sokanu: www.sokanu.com/discover
      2. U.S. Occupational Handbook: www.bls.gov/ooh/home.htm
5. Create an action plan.
   a. Create action steps for students: Action steps are a series of short, tangible assignments customized to fit the student's needs and the topics discussed during the meeting. We recommend that you copy and paste the tools previously mentioned as a general approach. However, depending on the conversation, the career coach has the discretion to add to the student's plan that goes beyond career discernment and development.
   b. Put action steps on a career coaching form: All action steps should appear on a career coaching form for tracking purposes so the career coach can track conversations and update progress.
   c. E-mail action steps: This keeps students from forgetting about the plan they devised during the meeting and helps to keep track of progress.
6. Assessment: Send students a brief survey on their career coaching experience.

self-reflection skills to create honest self-assessments related to their career goals. One way we do this is by asking students to complete a career skills self-assessment exercise (e.g., CareersPortal, n.d.), which invites them to reflect on their level of attainment of the top 10 skills currently in demand by employers. Once this is completed, participants are asked to reflect on which of these skills they have developed and to share some specific examples of how they used them. We also ask them to designate the top three skills they need to work on and to create an action plan to address them. Ideally, students complete this self-assessment at the end of their sophomore year so they can use the findings from it in the action planning during junior year.

Action: The Junior Experience

A big focus of the junior year is having students take part in career-focused experiential activities that can help them be more marketable after graduation. The emphasis for this year of their college career is taking career-related actions. Students in our target population are encouraged to participate in at least one internship experience in their junior year, and they are invited to engage in multiple networking experiences that range from participating in the university's alumni connections program to taking part in informational interviews with professionals in their fields. Through interactions with first-generation students, we were seeing students close to graduation who had never participated in an internship nor had any networking experience. We knew this was because first-generation students did not have time for career-focused activities because of their family obligations and career capital barriers they faced. Therefore, these structured experiences help build the type of career capital first-generation students often lack.

In addition, program participants are encouraged to meet with a career coach at least once during their junior year to discuss the progress they have made in their career planning and to reflect on their experiential career-related activities. It is extremely important to ensure that students are getting something from the career coaching experience. At the end of every career coaching meeting, we e-mail students a list of the action items they agreed to complete. As an example, after a meeting in the first part of the year, we might send the action items listed at the end of this chapter. We also include a link to a brief assessment of their experience in the career coaching meeting asking them to discuss their experience with the career coaching process, reflect on tangible applications of the content covered, and make suggestions to improve the career coaching experience. We were intentional in creating an assessment that was brief, to the point, and easy to complete.

Preparation: The Senior Experience

As we worked with Jennifer in her transition from DePaul to employment, we came to understand two very important challenges she was facing. First, she struggled to understand the tangible steps she needed to take to ensure she was graduating on time. For example, Jennifer did not know she needed to apply for graduation nor did she know that she needed to complete a degree audit to ensure that she met all the major requirements for her college. Second, Jennifer struggled with an overwhelming sense of loss at the thought of leaving a place she had come to love over her four years on campus.

The senior experience is focused on helping first-generation students with the transition out of the university. Although a part of this transition is to help students understand the graduation processes (applying for degree conferral, degree auditing, etc.) and to ensure they are actively engaged in postcollege planning (active job search, graduate school applications, etc.), a greater emphasis is placed on an "end of undergrad reflection" to help students process their transition from first-generation undergraduate students to first-generation graduate students or first-generation white-collar professionals.

These two distinct transition processes—to graduate school or a career—help students prepare for the next stage in their life, and they create closure for their undergraduate experience through structured reflective processes. We encourage students to develop a checklist within a specific timeline to ensure they are taking the necessary steps toward a successful postcollege experience. Additionally, we engage students in explicit reflection sessions that allow them to make meaning of their tenure at the university and help them understand the unique skills they have gained as a result of successfully navigating college as a first-generation student.

Although we came to this particular understanding with our first-generation graduating seniors, we realized reflection and closure were important and relevant for all our program participants. Because of this, we developed a senior transitions curriculum that focused on tangible to-dos as well as focused reflection. Students are encouraged to participate in at least three one-on-one meetings with a career coach, which allows us to engage them in this process. Alternatively, students can opt to participate in a senior retreat, which condenses the three-part meeting series into an all-day, off-campus experience. Figure 6.2 provides an example of a senior retreat schedule.

In addition, we have begun offering online career coaching opportunities to students through Skype or Google Hangout, which was particularly important given that the vast majority of our first-generation students and students of color were commuting an average of 30 minutes to and from campus. Additionally, we are moving toward providing career discernment online modules to allow students to work with the curriculum at their own

Figure 6.2 Senior retreat overview.

1. Day 1: Evening
   a. Check-ins and introductions
   b. Get-to-know-you activities
   c. Expectations and setting goals
2. Day 2: Morning
   a. Identifying and managing transition
   b. Developing skills for postcollege success
   c. Alumni panel: Life after college
3. Day 2: Afternoon
   a. Reflection: Alumni panel
   b. Postcollege success planning
   c. University resources for career-related success
   d. Closing activity: Sharing circle

pace. This benefits our commuter students who may come to campus only for their classes and first-generation students who are more likely to be at work during the times our services are offered.

Capturing Success: Early Career Alumni

Career centers across colleges and universities gather data to determine success through career and volunteer placement and graduate school matriculation, which is important for a myriad of reasons. Prospective students and their families seek information that will help them make the best decision possible, but it is equally important for us to ensure that we maintain an active connection with our graduates. By making an effort to stay connected to and interact with our early career alumni, we hope to provide networking opportunities for future program participants. For example, we encourage students to connect with our alumni association as well as our alumni mentoring program through the campus career center. During the last meeting we have with them in their senior year, we discuss the opportunities to give back to their campus community. We also encourage them to send us their first business card for contact information as potential mentors for undergraduate students.

If we can connect with them early in their career, we could keep them informed throughout their career, and they might be open to participating in some of the networking events and career transition programs we have developed. Ideally, we will be able to use alumni who went through the program as examples to encourage current students to participate in meaningful mentoring experiences to assist in building career capital.

Assessment: How Do You Know It Works?

To ensure that our students participate in strong career capital building and discernment experiences that also tie into a strong sense of identity consciousness, our team decided to integrate the systems theory framework (Arthur & McMahon, 2005) to serve as the identity-conscious foundation for our work. Therefore, students who participate in postcollege success initiatives can develop a career plan through exploration and involvement in various career-related opportunities and programs that encourage self-awareness and career discernment. To assess this, we decided to look at how career coaching, the service that demands the highest engagement and is the most personal, affects their career capital building, discernment, and their career development.

Career coaching is the most personal and holistic career capital and career discernment building experience students can have. Therefore, we decided to look at the impact of career coaching on three areas: students' ability to explain the importance of career capital, students' ability to use the concept of career capital to identify campus resources to help with their their career plans, and students' ability to use the career discernment process during career coaching to help them articulate their career plan in relation to their personal values and career needs.

We found the career coaching process did help students with their career discernment process and with finding and using the campus career center resources. However, one remaining question was, Did it change their behavior toward their career development planning? We responded to this question by creating more tangible tools and connections with the career center staff. Nonetheless, we learned that it is important to include questions or conduct follow-up focus groups to find out if students who experience career coaching actually changed their behavior to lead them to career success.

Conclusion

Six months after graduating, Jennifer stopped into the office while in town visiting her family. She updated us on her transition from the university and talked about how much she enjoyed the work she was doing. Jennifer also talked about how proud her family was of her, and even though they often asked when she was coming home, she felt she was able to navigate those conversations in a way that felt empowering.

As higher education professionals, we have a responsibility to ensure that our first-generation students and students of color are prepared for long-term career success. Given what we know specifically about these distinct populations, we need to understand that the foundation for their success should be built as early in their experiences as undergraduate students as possible to have the most impact on their career trajectory. We believe that adding an identity-conscious, career-related component to programs and individual interactions with students can add a tremendous amount of value to their experience with our offices and programs.

Action Items

As you begin to explore ways to incorporate career discernment experiences for students of color and first-generation college students into your program, it is important to take into consideration the ways their identities might affect their access to career capital. The following are some tangible action items and examples of ways to engage students of color and first-generation students through career discernment and career capital development processes.

1. Find out what career-related program currently exists and how it helps first-generation students and students of color. We encourage you to meet with personnel from campus offices that provide career-related programming or services to better understand not only what they offer but also how they serve first-generation students and students of color. Integrate their programming to create intentional experiences that focus on career capital and career discernment. For example, we created a year-long one-on-one career coaching curriculum that focuses on two areas: to help students understand how to use the career center and connect them with staff and to have career discernment discussions focus on holistic career decision making that incorporates their identity and family experiences. Ask these questions: Are these students interacting with career-related offices on campus? What barriers do our first-generation students face as they endure the career development process? What can we do to address those barriers?

2. Find groups of active sophomores who identify as first generation and students of color to participate in your new identity-focused career development programming. Many first-generation students and students of color who are active during their freshman year provide you with a recruiting pool of students for your postcollege success programming. For example, we recruit first-generation students and students of color in our first-year mentoring program for our sophomore career discernment

program. We encourage their mentors to promote the program as the next step in their college experience.

3. Start with sophomores and build on their experience. We found it helpful to start small. We began our efforts addressing an important issue we saw in our students and did research to determine the best way to address the sophomore slump many were experiencing. Once you have a solid group of sophomores, you can then work to develop the next experience for them in their junior year. As that first cohort of students make the transition into their junior year, you can then work to create their senior experience.

4. Work with your alumni office to determine what type of demographic data is collected. Demographic data from the alumni office can help determine the specific method of outreach to connect alumni with current students. If the office is not collecting that kind of data, you can make a case to begin doing so by showing the impact it can have on first-generation college students and students of color.

5. Observe and assess your services and programming through an identity-conscious lens. It has been important to us as we think about our work through the lens of identity consciousness to use that same lens to assess the impact of the program on the participants. Like most higher education practitioners, we continually assessed and observed how our services affected first-generation students and students of color. However, one of our strengths that allowed us to provide quality career development services was challenging ourselves to assess the program through an identity-conscious lens to create more innovative programming. Every year we hold staff retreats to review our work and find ways to be innovative when creating initiatives to help first-generation students achieve postcollege success. Keeping the identity-conscious conversation alive with your staff will help create strong career development programming and services to help first-generation students and students of color attain career capital, career self-efficacy, and, ultimately, career success.

References

Arthur, N., & McMahon, M. (2005). Multicultural career counseling: Theoretical applications of the systems theory framework. *Career Development Quarterly, 53,* 208–222.

CareersPortal. (n.d.). *Self-assessment tools.* Retrieved from http://www.careersportal.ie/careerplanning/self_assessment.php#.Vh7X3exVhBc

Constantine, M., & Flores, L. (2006). Psychological distress, perceived family conflict, and career development issues in college students of color. *Journal of Career Assessment, 14*(3), 354–369.

Rios-Aguilar, C., & Deil-Amen, R. (2012). Beyond getting in and fitting in: An examination of social networks and professionally relevant social capital among Latina/o university students. *Journal of Hispanic Higher Education, 11*(2), 179–196.

Schaller, M. (2005). Wandering and wondering: Traversing the uneven terrain of the second college year. *About Campus, 10*(3), 17–24.

7

EMPOWERMENT AGENTS

Developing Staff and Faculty to Support
Students at the Margins

Sumun L. Pendakur

P icture a newly minted graduate of a higher education or student affairs master's program. Maybe this graduate (or new professional) is you. You have lived a set of experiences and studied a curriculum that included an analysis of structural and systemic difference, power, and privilege as well as the stories of different communities in higher education. You vow that you will be a change agent in the field, serving the marginalized and pushing against the dominant structures that reinforce the status quo. You are cautiously optimistic that you will be able to weave your abilities and knowledge into the workplace in such a way that you will be asking critical questions and working to empower working-class students, first-generation students, and students of color—all while maintaining your own authenticity.

But what kind of a mind-set will you need to best form partnerships with marginalized students and question and challenge institutional structures all at the same time? What are the key skills you'll need to navigate institutional inertia, lack of resources, and your own position in the bureaucracy? You realize that as much as your program prepared you, helped you think through challenging concepts, and gave you the opportunity to hone a variety of skills, you haven't necessarily been trained to be a change agent. You are not alone. The vast majority of student affairs practitioners, from new professionals to senior leaders, have not received formal training in how to confront inequitable practices in higher education or how to mentor and work with marginalized students in ways that are truly empowering. Many learn skills along the way, which, combined with a critically conscious mind-set, lead to a set of practices that are transformative. But what if we had a road map to follow?

Overview

This chapter discusses empowerment agents (Stanton-Salazar, 1997, 2011) as models of thought and practice who call into question the race-blind, gender-blind standards of a meritocracy by naming and challenging the extant stratification in U.S. higher education. In our inequitable context, higher education institutions have not adopted practices and cultures to fully enable all students to succeed (Kezar, 2011). In fact, our higher education institutions (whether public, private, historically White, or majority minority) often end up rewarding those who bring with them higher levels of cultural and social capital, which are the knowledge, skill, and ability to form relationships that are situated as normative and valuable by the dominant society (Bourdieu, 1986). For example, expecting all students to willingly and readily visit professors during their office hours without making why and how explicit is dependent on socialization in the family/community/ system of schooling and ensures that those who know how to play the game will be rewarded by a system that is supposedly meritocratic. Now, combine this existing system of rewards with the deficit orientation of campus diversity discourses that construct working-class students or students of color as in need of compensatory or remedial programs (Iverson, 2007). These discourses and programs essentially suggest that working-class or minority students and families are responsible for a lack of success in academia because students enter school without the normative cultural knowledge and skills expected by the institution (Yosso, 2005). What does this combination mean? It means that the key assumption that guides the deficit framework and the status quo system of rewards is that it is not the institution that needs to change or evolve but rather the working-class or minority students themselves. The problem then lies with the student rather than with the system that was inequitably structured in the first place.

Given these inequities, staff and faculty have the opportunity to serve as empowerment agents to have an impact on the lives of students on the margins while also challenging the university from the inside. I suggest in this chapter that faculty and staff can be agents of change and create empowerment from within but only by adopting a reflective, identity-conscious framework that actively grapples with the hegemonic nature of power, inside and outside our institutions of learning. My work with the empowerment agent framework emerges from my doctoral research. A number of educational researchers have focused their work on students, such as student success models, the value of particular types of interactions and interventions, and student development theories. However, as Bensimon (2007) points out, higher education professionals are missing from the picture. She refers to the dearth of scholarly research and practical consideration to truly understand how one's own knowledge bases, value systems, experiences, and abilities directly affect how students experience the educational environment.

My research, therefore, focused on transformational agents in elite higher education institutions, their belief systems and worldview development, how they translated beliefs into practice, the multidirectional ways successful agents changed students and the institution, and how they maintained critical consciousness and persisted in the face of fatigue and formidable barriers to change. Drawing on my original research as well as the social capital frameworks of Bourdieu (1986), Lin (2001), and Stanton-Salazar (1997, 2004, 2011), I aim to provide a best practices road map for staff and faculty to think through the knowledge, skills, and tools necessary to actively embed identity—as well as all the related facets of power, privilege, access, and assets—into their work as transformational agents in higher education. It is ultimately not enough to ask that programs and interventions change and evolve; we as practitioners must accept the challenge of identity-conscious approaches to student success. As one of my study participants explained, thinking critically about the success of students who have traditionally been marginalized in higher education requires a conscious act and the ability to take a stand:

> If we're talking about changing this place, you can't have a chorus of people saying the same thing, especially when it's not based in fact. I think you have to have people to stand up on the side of truth. Even when it's unpopular, even when it's controversial. I mean, history has shown us that our great leaders in the past all had their moments when they have to take similar stances. . . . It all starts when somebody was able to stand up and say, "Look, this is not right; this is problematic." That's why I feel it is important to say it. (Pendakur, 2010, p. 76)

In the following pages, I briefly discuss some of the theories and models underlying my research. Next, I explain the road map I mentioned earlier, that is, the fundamental beliefs and mind-set necessary for you to engage in transformative work as well as key actions and practices that will enable you to serve as a successful empowerment agent.

Chapter Framework

This chapter is particularly informed by social capital theory (Bourdieu, 1986; Dika & Singh, 2002; Lin, 2001) and theories on institutional/empowerment agents (Bensimon, 2007; Stanton-Salazar, 1997, 2011). Social capital theory is the foundational school of thought behind many researchers' attempts to explain educational disparities as disaggregated by race, class, gender, ethnicity, and immigrant status (Lareau, 2001; Lareau & Horvat, 1999; Stanton-Salazar, 1997, 2001). The seminal scholar Bourdieu (1986) makes the case that institutional normative bias mirrors and rewards the social or cultural capital of the upper (dominant) classes and undervalues the norms and behaviors of the working class. This bias directly contributes to the reproduction of systemic inequities (especially in regard to race, class, and gender variables). Bourdieu and Lin suggest that the resources that represent social capital are embedded in social relations, not just in the individual, and that the societal distribution of these resources results in structural embeddedness. Although the resources of social capital are not located within the individual, the ability to access and use them lies with the individual. The awareness of these resources and skills becomes paramount for the individual who wishes to engage in the work of transformative relationship building and change. An example of the importance of this awareness is in the realm of the practitioner's ability to identify and skillfully distribute resources in his or her network, particularly to working-class students of color, and to challenge the status quo of the institution.

Stanton-Salazar (2004) explains that mobilizing social capital networks (social connections) for purposeful action occurs within the context of structural inequity in which the imbalance of power is normalized and within an economy in which valuable resources are distributed in an inequitable fashion. In the milieu of higher education, a context in which hierarchical relationships of privilege and power are the norm, many misinterpret academic (and other) success as directly related to the internalization of "appropriate" identities, norms, and values. According to Stanton-Salazar (1997), "Social antagonisms and divisions existing in the wider society operate to problematize . . . minority children's access to opportunities and resources that are . . . taken-for-granted products of middle-class family, community, and school networks" (p. 3). Because of an overreliance on the normative school of thought by institutions and educators, students are left to decode the hidden curriculum on their own. Stanton-Salazar (2011) therefore defines *empowerment agents* as individuals who leverage their positions and capacities to either directly transmit or negotiate access to highly prized, key forms of institutional resources, support, and opportunities while concurrently working to alter the institution from the inside. The network orientation of a successful empowerment agent is centered on the critical idea that empowering marginalized students is not accomplished only through the actions of an individual but is built in concert with actors, resources, and support mechanisms embedded in their own social networks and bridging functions (Lin, 2001; Stanton-Salazar, 2011). For working-class minority college students without preexisting ties or a predeveloped ability to find their way in a system that is predicated on White middle-class norms, developing ties to empowerment agents becomes a crucial means of accessing institutional support, learning to decode institutionally sanctioned discourse, navigating healthy development, and participating in power. Bensimon (2007) additionally defined these agents as individuals who possess sensitivity, training, and an expertise that enables them to be receptive and helpful to marginalized students.

In the structurally inequitable world of higher education, empowerment agents are critically important because of their active choice to provide institutional support to low-status students as part of a committed agenda (Stanton-Salazar, 1997). Because of the explicit and strategic nature of empowerment agents—their consciousness regarding structural inequity and their actions to counterbalance inequity—their work with minority youth becomes counterhegemonic.

Identity Consciousness

If a staff or faculty member chooses to serve as an empowerment agent, the active consideration of multiple facets of identity as well as an ideological motivation for doing the work of counterstratification is a requirement. To mentor or to create programmatic interventions or to teach without this thoughtful, critical approach often serves to reify the dominant norms of the institution (that reflect White, male, middle-class norms). Without a commitment to a radical transformation of the culture of power, privilege, and inequity, the best intentions of agents could lead simply to additional social reproduction rather than a fundamental shift in our educational and societal systems (Stanton-Salazar, 1997, 2011). Being an empowerment agent is more than writing a recommendation letter or mentoring or securing an internship for a student of color. These actions are important, but they are also focused on the individual only. In other words, working with working-class minority students to help them decode the hidden curriculum and navigate the system of education may lead only to individual mobility and success as well as to a relatively uncritical assimilation into the status quo. Individual success and a faux meritocracy are hallmarks of neoliberal measures of accomplishment. A pedagogical commitment to destabilizing the normative halls of academia and structures of inequity as well as direct action that runs counter to societal pressure and reproductive forces is necessary to transform the very consciousness of those whom the empowerment agent supports. Stanton-Salazar (2011) defines the *empowerment agent* as one who enables youths to "decode the system," to momentarily disembed from the environment, engage in a critical moral dialogue with it, and to seek opportunities for working collaboratively to change the sociopolitical context" (p. 26). An ideal empowerment agent not only offers working-class students or students of color access to institutional support but also alters their destinies by empowering them with a critical consciousness (ideological mind-set) and the means (tools for action) to transform themselves and society (Stanton-Salazar, 2011). Critical consciousness (Freire, 1970) represents a twofold process of understanding the oppressive and contradictory world around us and taking action against the hegemonic elements that are illuminated by that understanding.

In summary, to serve as an empowerment agent requires staff or faculty members to have critically examined their own identity and their own relationship to power and privilege and to have worked to create a resourced social capital network of relationships for the benefit of marginalized students. In addition, the successful practitioner will have learned key skills to navigate institutional roadblocks as well as continually question the status quo norms of our campuses (and teach those questioning skills). So how does all this happen in the face of institutional repression, bureaucratic pressures, prestige maximization efforts, and other externalized and internalized barriers?

The next section delves into the key beliefs and attributes that are necessary to truly engage in transformative, identity-conscious work. I follow with examples of specific actions and practices of successful empowerment agents.

From Theory to Practice: A Road Map

The following pages cover two areas as a primer for becoming an empowerment agent: key beliefs and attributes and counterstratifying practices and actions. A number of key beliefs and attributes are essential to good practice of successful empowerment agents. First and foremost is the care and affirmation of marginalized students situated in a social justice worldview. Just knowing that a student is a working-class student of color does not necessarily offer a prescription for a plan of action. Taking the time to invest in students' journeys and their interests and choices while serving as a guide, mentor, and counterstratification source is critical to authentic empowerment. The next pages explore critical network orientation, asset mindedness, community embeddedness, holding a political worldview, and maintaining critical consciousness in the face of status quo practices. Following an exploration of necessary beliefs, we delve into empowering actions for you and actions that teach students to decode and navigate the system as well as challenge it.

Key Beliefs: Critical Network Orientation

Going back to the idea of social capital as resources that are accessible through relationships, it is paramount to develop a strong network orientation with key relationships horizontally and vertically inside and outside the institution with those who hold resources and share a commitment to marginalized students (personally or intellectually). An example of this comes from one of my study participants:

> You do need to be able to pick up the phone and call on somebody with confidence. To know that you have a faculty member [who's] in your corner who understands the work that you do and is willing to work with you to better serve a low-income or first-generation student is invaluable. So absolutely, relationships are key.

In a context in which students with higher cultural capital tend to receive attention from their professors because they possess the markers of skills and language valued in academia, the structure, resourcefulness, and vitality of your own social networks will be valuable to your practice as an empowerment agent because they enhance your ability to access and redistribute resources for the benefit of marginalized students.

Key Beliefs: Asset Mindedness

In addition to a critical network orientation, one of the most crucial factors in serving as an empowerment agent is your own perception of working-class students of color. You must be able to challenge deficit-minded perspectives (Bensimon, 2007) or culture of poverty perspectives about working-class students of color. Emerging from the mid-1960s, the notions of cultural deficit encompass theories that minorities are culturally deficient (as opposed to the White majority.) The culture of poverty, popularized by Moynihan (1965), was based on Lewis's (1959) concept that the poor (particularly the urban poor) have a unique value system that keeps them poor. Deficit models do not place the responsibility for change and adaptation on the institution or the system but rather on the shoulders of the marginalized. Successful empowerment agents hold an asset-based orientation to working-class students of color. Describing a type of asset often overlooked in academia, one study participant said:

> I think that these students are far more committed to giving back and improving opportunities and life chances of those who are disadvantaged than our general students. I think many of these students come with a stronger sense of who they are. Whether that's because people have constantly tried to define them, I don't know, but they tend to come with a stronger sense of who they are. (Pendakur, 2010, p. 67)

Acknowledging and centering students' lived experiences, sense of identity, and community commitments as strengths are vital tools. The process of thinking about key assets marginalized students bring with them to the college environment and applying those assets to increase student success rather than only focusing on deficits is a hallmark of a strong empowerment agent.

Key Beliefs: Community Embeddedness

In addition to possessing an asset orientation, Stanton-Salazar (2011) explains that a central role of the empowerment agent is to engage working-class minority youths in transforming the world around them by enacting meaningful social change encompassing a variety of actions. These actions include collaborating with others, acting politically, contesting oppressive institutional policies and practices, working to solve community-based problems, and taking up democratic leadership. For empowerment agents to take on this influential role in the lives of marginalized students, a complex vision of community and interdependence is required. Applying a culturally grounded meaning of community by connecting it to your work with marginalized students on a daily basis is necessary and challenges the status quo. Prioritizing community advancement in its totality rather than just prodding one's students toward individual achievement is the goal.

As one study participant said:

> I think that relative to my [community's] culture, American culture tends to be very individualistic. It's about individual achievement. It's the complete opposite to our culture, which is about the community. Even if an individual succeeds, how are they going to use that success to benefit the community? That question very much informs the person that I am today and the work that I do. It's a message that I constantly remind my students of. Okay, you are successful, you've been afforded very, very privileged opportunities. How you are going to use these opportunities to better the lives of others? How are you going to get back to your community? Or providing that message of, "Don't forget where you came from because your community needs you. They are depending on you and your success." You didn't get here by yourself. People helped you along the way to get to this point. How are you going to repay those people or repay your community? I think we advance or we progress as individuals, but we have to go back to our communities and make sure our communities are moving forward as well. So that's a very big aspect of my cultural philosophy and my professional philosophy as well. (Pendakur, 2010, p. 73)

I highlight this particular set of attributes, convictions about creating community and giving back, as a centrally important belief set for empowerment agents. Creating community is philosophical, based on place, and related to shared struggles and a sense of interdependence. Creating community challenges the individualistic orthodoxy of American neoliberalism. In the same way, giving back is about moving beyond individual gain and success to thinking critically about the community from which you come, how multiple communities' stories intersect, and how moving forward must include advancing your community. The community-oriented philosophies and lived experiences of empowerment agents help them translate a social justice mind-set or critical consciousness to the marginalized students they seek to empower.

Key Beliefs: A Political Worldview

Equally important to the previously mentioned key beliefs is an ability to live the worldview and belief system in all contexts and take a broad (and long) approach to engagement. Your worldview must necessarily be political and able to weather a lifelong commitment. The process of making higher education institutions more equitable and less stratified is a political act, as described by one of the study participants:

> This, the movement for institutional equity, is a constant political process with people who are against what you are trying to do. And then, there are the people who will say that they are for it, but actually never do anything to make it happen. And to me, that's actually much more important than any single event along the way. It's more of the commitment to that issue from the beginning to the very end of life; that's what I most value about the whole thing. It's a whole political commitment over a long period of time from a number of different positions where I have learned a lot. And to me, that's one political movement. I do consider making these universities more responsive to be a political act. (Pendakur, 2010, p. 76)

Thinking in political terms about one's worldview is necessary for an empowerment agent who wishes to work with the process of change over his or her lifespan, regardless of a specific position or title. In addition, developing a keen understanding of institutional politics is a useful tool. Taking the time to better understand campus dynamics and know which peers you can trust and whom you can call on as allies is time well spent. The combination of political understanding with key cross-institutional relationships increases your ability to be effective for the students you wish to serve and empower.

Key Beliefs: Maintaining Critical Consciousness

Finally, the empowerment agent must maintain critical consciousness while embedded in the power structure of the institution. You must balance your critical consciousness, your multiplicity of networks, and your community-based commitments in the face of a dominant institutional narrative. The temptation to simply follow the status quo is incredibly powerful, as is institutional inertia, bureaucratic roadblocks, and the sheer power of hegemony, which can wear down even the most equity-minded practitioner. But maintaining a high level of reflectivity and reflexivity is a key strategy to resist co-optation by the very system you wish to change. Successful empowerment agents actively contemplate and examine their life, work, positionality, and relationships. They spend time thinking through beliefs, privilege, patterns of practice, and their own subjectivity. Reflexivity refers to the praxis-oriented, bidirectional relationship between reflection and action. An empowerment agent's reflexivity leads to greater recognition of his or her place in an inequitable system and to further action against institutional hegemony. That action leads to reflection, and the cycle continues.

We have explored five key beliefs and attributes of empowerment agents. This counterstratifying mind-set is important because although actions such as mentoring, advising, or resourcing come with excellent intentions, the outcome is too often reproductive, individualistic, and does not challenge the status quo. That being said, mind-set and beliefs without action don't involve the system or empower the student. The following section explores key practices successful empowerment agents employ in working with marginalized students, followed by a discussion of ways to teach decoding and challenge the system.

Counterstratifying Ways of Working With Students

Any faculty or staff member who takes a mentoring approach to his or her work with students will offer support through advising, letters of recommendation, introductions to people in their networks, and more. Beyond these expected forms of support, the following are some of the various practices and interventions my study participants used in their work with marginalized students, ranging from classroom pedagogy to generating specific resources to engaging in select mentoring and empowering behaviors:

- mentoring, advising, and serving as an advocate;
- minimizing the impact of transfer shock;
- connecting students to key figures and resources so they can build their own networks of people who share a philosophical commitment to increasing access and offering institutional support for working-class students of color;

- actively seeking marginalized students to mentor;
- developing a long-term commitment to student journeys in which strengths are acknowledged;
- constructing equitable curricular and cocurricular spaces where the experiences and stories of marginalized communities are given centrality;
- using classroom time for all students to explore and understand power and cultural capital;
- developing one's office as a safe space; and
- building confidence in students by invoking their valuable forms of knowledge that are not always acknowledged. (Pendakur, 2010)

An example of the combination of mind-set and practice that is being discussed can be seen in one participant's description of the way he prioritizes marginalized students:

I give these students the highest priority, and I literally think of it that way. I have done this from the very beginning. If you are an underrepresented minority, if you are a first-generation college student, if you are low income, I want to see you in my office as opposed to anybody else. And the reason I do this is because I think I am balancing out what are usually much more distant faculty. I mean, the vast majority of faculty are not minority, are not first-generation college graduates, are not low income. So for me, it's trying to do that balancing. For example, when I am teaching the big courses, I instruct each of my TAs [teaching assistants] as to my priorities because I want to know the students who fall into these categories so that I can encourage them. My TAs can help identify students for me. Particularly if they are either struggling or if they are strong, to take advantage of research. I take particular joy in working with those students. (Pendakur, 2010, p. 165)

Empowerment agents aim to create a holistic atmosphere of support, push, and success for marginalized students. Whether inside or outside the classroom, a successful agent aids students in developing coping strategies such as help-seeking orientations, problem-solving abilities, networking skills, and behaviors directed toward overcoming institutional barriers (Stanton-Salazar, 2011). Whether in the interpersonal environment or in the classroom-based context, it is important to strategically help marginalized students think critically about a network orientation as well as larger systemic questions of power, enabling them to develop agency in an inequitable system.

Decoding and Challenging

In addition to the practical, yet counterstratifying relationship-building and skill-building actions described in the preceding section, the empowerment agent works with students to decode (navigate) the system and challenge and change the system. These two major functions differentiate the good-hearted practitioner from the effective empowerment agent. Decoding the system may involve unlocking the hidden curriculum, achieving one's goals within an existing system while learning what structures need to be dismantled, navigating channels of power, and accessing key institutional resources and forms of support. A practitioner whose mind-set and orientation are driven by empowerment can work with students to help them navigate and challenge the institution in a counterproductive and counterexclusionary way. Some examples of teaching decoding and skills for challenging from within include

- being explicit and teaching the tacit knowledge that is taken for granted among privileged populations, such as financial education and networking skills;
- exposing the hidden curriculum through a process of explanation, demonstration, and breaking down complexities;
- role-modeling how to navigate the system with integrity;
- being students' ally on the inside by helping them to better comprehend institutional politics and demands;
- helping students develop the skills to be heard by those in power in the institution;
- helping students build issue-based understanding, or solidarity, with other students and other campus- and community-based movements to foment collective change; and
- capitalizing on the community-oriented feelings among marginalized students to help them think beyond individual achievement as the marker of success. (Pendakur, 2010)

One of my study participants explained this process of decoding, navigating, and challenging eloquently:

> One of my mentors once said in order to play the game, you need to learn the rules . . . so that later you can bend them or break them. You have to learn the language, and every institution, every organization has a certain language. And once you know the language, then you can help interpret. You can speak their code, you can extend their metaphor and you can slowly, but surely, be an agent of change. But if you have no idea what the

language is, there is no way you can begin. You will spin your wheels, you will get on your one soapbox that no one relates to, and you can't really be an agent of change. You can change *your* immediate situation, change yourself and change your plight, but in the process maybe has left sort of a sour feeling, so that after you are through, they close the door behind you and lock it up. So you can't jump in and create waves without understanding, without knowing the power players, and understanding the structure. (Pendakur, 2010, p. 147)

This understanding of the underlying inequities in higher education as well as the will, skills, and resources that affect student experiences differentiates the empowerment agent from the standard practitioner. Teaching tacit knowledge through clear explanations of assignments, unambiguous expectations on syllabi, directly tapping marginalized students and inviting them to meetings during office hours, and making processes (e.g., dissertation writing) more transparent are but a few tools at the disposal of faculty members who wish to serve as empowerment agents. Faculty and staff can model the critique of the dominant system and teach students through a process of theorizing how to creatively play the game and tackle the system. You can teach students to navigate the institution and its demands while helping them to think critically about hierarchy, access, and privilege. At the same time, aiding students to better comprehend institutional politics and demands and build coalitions on issues of solidarity are equally important skills to teach. Forming partnerships with students to develop institutionally savvy forms of resistance is a powerful act. Finally, your own reflection on undergraduate and graduate school experiences and acknowledgment of the impact of empowerment agents on your own life and daily practices are valuable. This reflection enables you keep counterstratification at the heart of your work in building relationships with marginalized students.

The praxis-oriented empowerment agent combines a set of key beliefs, reflexivity, and a strong network with the ability to engage in counterstratifying actions on behalf of marginalized students while empowering them to successfully decode, navigate, and challenge the very system that renders them vulnerable.

Assessment: How Do You Know It Works?

This chapter does not focus on a specific programmatic intervention but rather on developing the mind-sets, skills, and attributes to fundamentally alter the experiences of marginalized students in higher education through an intersectional, identity-conscious, counterstratifying approach to retention and student success. Your role as an empowerment agent fits into a constellation of efforts—programmatic, institutional, and structural. Therefore, serving as an empowerment agent still begs the same questions: What does success look like? How do you know if you were successful?

I recommend two resources for self-assessment (and institutional assessment): the equity scorecard (Harris & Bensimon, 2007) and the National Association of Diversity Officers in Higher Education (NADOHE) standards of professional practice (Worthington, Stanley, & Lewis, 2014). The equity scorecard is a practical, hands-on tool and process that encourages the kind of reflective and reflexive practice described earlier in this chapter. The scorecard is designed to facilitate ongoing learning as well as a concurrent change in mind-set and behavior among practitioners. The equity scorecard helps staff and faculty adopt an evidence-based approach to increasing awareness of race-based inequities in higher education as well as developing a sense of responsibility to address the extant gaps. Harris and Bensimon write, "The equity scorecard provides the means and the context for institutional leaders to develop color-consciousness and thereby build their capacities to assess and respond to race-based disparities in student outcomes" (p. 83). Critically, the authors are careful to point out that "institutional leaders" are not just those with positional power, but rather "just about any campus professional whose beliefs, knowledge, and practices can affect the outcomes of minority students" (p. 80). All of us can be central to the process of individual and structural change.

Given the ongoing training and exploration of empowerment to which agent has to commit as well as the depth of reflectivity and reflexivity required, I also recommend the standards of professional practice developed by the National Association of Chief Diversity Officers (NADOHE; Worthington, Stanley, & Lewis, 2014) as a strong tool for self-assessment. Although not all of you reading this book aim to be chief diversity officers, the NADOHE standards offer a comprehensive set of benchmarks to assess your knowledge, skills, and gaps to adopt a continual growth and learning model for yourself. Embedded in the 12 standards are guideposts, such as Standard 3: "Understands the contexts, cultures, and politics within institutions that impact the implementation and management of effective diversity change efforts" (p. 231). Standard 11 urges the practitioner to have a "current and historical knowledge related to issues of nondiscrimination, access, and equity in higher education institutions" (p. 232). Some of the standards may or may not apply to your daily work or interactions, but, for example, thinking strategically about your role in the contextual web of your campus while developing a depth of understanding of historically and structurally rooted discrimination and bias will aid you in your goal to serve as an authentic and transformative empowerment agent. Meld the NADOHE (2014) standards with Bensimon's (2007) urgings to push against deficit-based thinking in higher education, incorporate Bourdieu's (1986) progressive conceptualization of social capital, and explore Stanton-Salazar's (1997, 2011) articulations of the potential and power of your own transformational role on our campuses. Ask tough questions of yourself and of your institution.

Conclusion

For many of you reading this chapter, the call to work in higher education is deeply personal. Maybe you were a first-generation college student trying to figure out the campus culture and your professors' unspoken expectations. Maybe you were a student of color at a historically White institution who still winces when you think about the microaggressions you experienced in and outside the classroom on a regular basis. No matter the path of your own journey, all of you work in educational environments that have been structured to benefit those with the cultural and social capital deemed valid by a system laced with dominance and subordination. As I wrote earlier in the chapter, it is not enough to ask for programs and interventions to evolve. It is most certainly not enough to continue to use deficit-oriented frameworks that demand that the student adapt, not the institution. We as staff and faculty must be central to the creation of an alternative reality, one in which conscientious practitioners are not agents of a stratified system but agents of change and transformation.

The intellectual framing and practice-oriented road map I have provided in this chapter emerged from a very personal investigation into what was formerly a theoretical concept of the empowerment agent. I was looking for inspiration and guidance from grassroots activists, embedded change agents, social justice advocates, and more who shared the same aim: to challenge the very institution they served while empowering the students rendered subordinate by the institution itself. As the great abolitionist orator Frederick Douglass wrote in 1849,

> If there is no struggle there is no progress. . . . This struggle may be a moral one; or it may be a physical one; or it may be both moral and physical; but it must be a struggle. Power concedes nothing without demand. It never did and it never will. (Douglass, 1991)

In addition to developing and holding core sets of beliefs and engaging in counterstratifying practices, understanding the reproductive power of status quo practices, and your own vital role in the struggle for change, is key to your success as a transformative agent in higher education. The personal is political, just as the political is personal. I look forward to sharing this journey with you.

Action Items

1. Expand your investigation of your own understanding of institutional reproduction and hegemony as well as your own relationship to power, privilege, and identity to develop a reflective, reflexive, and counterstratifying mind-set.
2. Continue to develop a critical network orientation, asset mindedness, community embeddedness, a political worldview, and the ability to maintain critical consciousness while embedded in the power structure of your institution.
3. Engage in empowering actions and relationship building with students while also working with them to decode and navigate as well as challenge the educational system.
4. Periodically evaluate your own ability to do the work of an empowerment agent using assessment frameworks, tools, and processes at your disposal.

References

Bensimon, E. M. (2007). The underestimated significance of practitioner knowledge in the scholarship of student success. *Review of Higher Education, 30*(4), 441–469.

Bourdieu, P. (1986). The forms of capital. In J. G. Richardson (Ed.), *Handbook of theory and research for the sociology of education* (pp. 241–258). New York, NY: Greenwood Press.

Dika, S., & Singh, K. (2002). Applications of social capital in educational literature: A critical synthesis. *Review of Education Research, 72*(1), 31–60.

Douglass, F. (1991). Letter to an abolitionist associate. In K. Bobo, J. Kendall, & S. Max (Eds.), *Organizing for social change: A mandate for activity in the 1990s.* Washington, DC: Seven Locks Press.

Freire, P. (1970). *Pedagogy of the oppressed.* New York, NY: Continuum.

Harris, F., III, & Bensimon, E. M. (2007). The equity scorecard: A collaborative approach to assess and respond to racial/ethnic disparities in student outcomes. *New Directions for Student Services, 120*, 77–84.

Iverson, S. (2007). Camouflaging power and privilege: A critical race analysis of university diversity policies. *Educational Administration Quarterly, 43*(5), 586–611.

Kezar, A. (Ed.). (2011). *Recognizing and serving low-income students in higher education: An examination of institutional policies, practices, and culture.* New York, NY: Routledge.

Lareau, A. (2001). Linking Bourdieu's concept of capital to the broader field: The case of family-school relationships. In B. J. Biddle (Ed.), *Social class, poverty, and education: Policy and practice* (pp. 77–100). New York, NY: RoutledgeFalmer.

Lareau, A. & Horvat, E. M. (1999). Moments of social inclusion and exclusion: Race, class, and cultural capital in family-school relationships. *Sociology of Education, 72*(1), 37–53.

Lin, N. (2001). *Social capital: A theory of social structure and action.* New York, NY: Cambridge University Press.

Lewis, O. (1959). *Five families: Mexican case studies in the culture of poverty.* New York, NY: Basic Books.

Moynihan, D. (1965). *The Negro family: The case for national action.* Retrieved from www.dol.gov/oasam/programs/history/webid-meynihan.htm

Pendakur, S. L. (2010). *The search for transformative agents: The counter-institutional positioning of faculty and staff at an elite university.* Retrieved from digitallibrary.usc.edu/cdm/ref/collection/p15799coll127/id/421604

Stanton-Salazar, R. (1997). A social capital framework for understanding the socialization of racial minority children and youths. *Harvard Educational Review, 67*(1), 12–40.

Stanton-Salazar, R. (2001). *Manufacturing hope and despair: The school support networks of U.S.-Mexican youth.* New York, NY: Teachers College Press.

Stanton-Salazar, R. (2004). Social capital among working-class minority students. In M. A. Gibson, P. Gándara, & J. P. Koyama (Eds.), *School connections: U.S. Mexican youth, peers, and school achievement,* (pp. 18–38). New York, NY: Teachers College Press.

Stanton-Salazar, R. D. (2011). A social capital framework for the study of institutional agents and their role in the empowerment of low-status students and youth. *Youth & Society, 11*(43), 1066–1109.

Worthington, R. L., Stanley, C. A., & Lewis Sr., W. T. (2014). National Association of Diversity Officers in Higher Education standards of professional practice for chief diversity officers. *Journal of Diversity in Higher Education, 7*(4), 227–234.

Yosso, T. J. (2005). Whose culture has capital? A critical race theory discussion of community cultural wealth. *Race Ethnicity and Education, 8*(1), 69–91.

8

FOOD, SHELTER, AND SUCCESS

Mitigating Risk for Low-Income College Students

Art Munin and Michele Enos

H aving lost his job and home within the last month, Jacob was living in his car on the south side of Chicago, commuting daily to his private university. Each day started with a long ride on public transit, a shower at the campus recreation center, and a trip to the student center to see what events would be serving food that day—then Jacob finally headed off to class. With neither family nor friends and nowhere else to turn, Jacob's college career was his only source of focus and direction.

When a staff member in the dean of students office asked Jacob why he didn't at least drive his car closer to campus to cut down on his commute time, Jacob replied simply that his car was in the neighborhood where he grew up. It was home, and he felt more comfortable there.

Low-income students like Jacob are an invisible and greatly underserved population at colleges and universities throughout the United States. As his story shows and the title of this chapter suggests, food and shelter are some of the most foundational needs that foster the success of this student population. However, the impediments these students experience along their academic journeys can be so basic, they escape the attention of higher education administrators.

Overview

In this chapter we outline the varying hurdles many low-income college students encounter, including economic instability, mounting debt, homelessness, and food insecurity. We also explore tangible examples of what administrators can do to assist these students in substantive ways.

Chapter Framework

The framework on which this chapter is based is quite simple: students who are hungry; homeless; economically disadvantaged; and, overall, struggling to survive may be unable to achieve optimal success in their higher education pursuits. Maslow's (1943) hierarchy of needs clearly denotes that baseline requirements for physiological essentials as well as safety and security necessities must be met for people to pursue higher order goals. Of course, some individuals may be able to experience higher order success despite deficiencies, but their success can be hard fought and not reflect their optimal capacity. This circles back to the premise of this chapter: If higher education institutions are going to admit low-income college students, it is incumbent on colleges and universities to design services to help them succeed.

Identity Consciousness

In the effort to increase economic diversity on college campuses, universities must begin to fully understand the identity of a low-income student. Beyond the monetary needs of this student population, Baxter and Britton (2001) explain that the changes low-income students undergo at college have a significant effect not only on their sense of self but also on relationships with friends and family who still live in the world these students left behind. As seen in Jacob's story, low-income students' experiences are varied and nuanced and often go beyond a university's offering more financial aid. Class-based aspects of a student's identity shape his or her college experience in a variety of ways, and it is necessary for an institution of higher education to take this into account to holistically support this growing population (Aries & Seider, 2005). As we discuss later in this chapter, a variety of interventions and support systems that take into account campus culture must be put into place to adequately support the inherently diverse population of low-income students.

Ultimately, gaining access to our institutions is not sufficient to ensure success. We contend strongly that given the right support, low-income students can achieve optimal success in higher education and beyond. However, as outlined in the remainder of this chapter, colleagues across academia must learn more about who these students are, the intricacies of their struggles, and the options available to provide them with support on their higher education journey.

Understanding and Supporting Low-Income College Students: A Current Snapshot

Sara Martinez Tucker (2014) stated that "only 30 percent of low-income students enroll in college right after high school" (para. 1). That amounts to 4.5 million low-income, first-generation students in higher education, about 24% of our student population. As recently as 2013, only one in five low-income students who enroll in college will complete a baccalaureate degree by the age of 24 (Korn, 2015). By age 25, about 50% of students from high-income families have attained a bachelor's degree, but for low-income students the figure is only about 10% ("Increasing College Opportunity," 2014).

Low-income students depend on financial aid to keep their higher education dreams alive. Since 2008 the amount of aid dispensed by the federal government in the form of grants and loans has notably increased. While that can be positive, it means that the amount of student debt has also increased. In constant 2011 dollars, the total amount of student loan debt owned by the federal government in 2007 was $101 billion. That figure multiplied rapidly, jumping to $516 billion by 2012. Factoring in all forms of student debt (e.g., private loans), the debt carried by our college students as of 2012 was $956 billion. From 2000 to 2011, the average amount of student loans jumped by 39% (Aud et al., 2013). To some, these figures may just be numbers on a page, but to students like Alejandra Lalama, student loan debt is a lived reality (McCollum, 2014).

In November 2005 Alejandra Lalama thought her dream of becoming an audio engineer was beginning to become reality after she was accepted into a for-profit school in Florida that specializes in music, video, and film production. After meeting with a financial aid counselor from the university, Lalama's mother, a single parent and teacher, paid the $650 application fee and deposit. Eight years and $65,000 of student loan debt later, Lalama lives with her mother and works for an Internet service provider, spending almost her entire paycheck to pay back her school loans. Each month, she pays more than $750 toward this debt; however, with compounded interest, only $4,360.14 of the $32,000 she has paid has gone toward her principal balance (McCollum, 2014). Unfortunately Lalama's story is representative of the experience of many low-income students in higher education today.

Since the early 1980s college tuition and fees have increased at four times the rate of inflation, faster than even health care expenses. This means that the percentage of family income needed to pay for college has also increased. This and another factor, a growing disparity in income equality, have significantly affected low-income families. Within the last 30 years, the lowest income families in the United States have seen their earnings decrease by 7%, as opposed to families in the highest income bracket, who have seen their earnings rise by 73% (Cruz, Engle, & Lynch, 2011). Furthermore, a change in federal financial aid practices has also helped to widen this gap.

One of the most well-known federal government programs that supplies monetary aid to students with the most financial need, the Pell Grant, has seen a decline. In budget debates, policymakers have focused on ways to control the growth of the Pell Grant program, directly limiting low-income students' ability to receive this assistance. At the same time, a similar trend has been occurring in state governments as direct funding to institutions and grant aid to students has failed to keep pace with rising enrollments, which has directly led to tuition increases. In contrast, state grants not based on need have grown at triple the rate of need-based grants within the last 10 years (Cruz et al., 2011). This means that after exhausting all sources of grant aid, the typical low-income student must come up with more than $11,000 a year to attend a public or private nonprofit college. Every year, low-income families must pay or borrow nearly 75% of their family income for one of their children to attend a college or university. This is in direct contrast to middle-class families, who typically have to pay 27% of their family's income a year for higher education, or high-income families who only have to pay 14% (Cruz et al., 2011).

Acute Risk: Homeless Students in Higher Education

When school lets out for winter break, most students are excited to go home and spend time with friends and family. However, after completing her first semester at Salem State University, Tina Giarla wasn't thinking about visiting friends and family at all. Instead, she was worried about not only where she would live for the next month but also where she would live once she returned to school.

> It felt like my past was creeping up on me again. . . . I worked two-and-a-half-jobs and went to school full-time. I had to save extra money to rent a hotel in the case of an emergency so I wouldn't have to go to a shelter. It wasn't a comfortable feeling. (Gross, 2013, para. 6)

Giarla's experience in higher education is not unique. The Free Application for Federal Student Aid (FAFSA) estimates there are about 58,000 homeless students on campuses nationwide (Gross, 2013), but this number is only an estimate of a growing population because colleges are not currently required to keep track of their homeless students. Furthermore, counselors working with homeless youths in high schools and colleges confirm these figures go unreported because of the stigma attached to homelessness (Cortes & Munin, 2014). At many institutions, residence halls close during winter break, some even for Thanksgiving and spring break. Often the only on-campus option during these time periods for students who live on campus like Giarla is to pay additional money to stay in the residence halls or find somewhere else to stay temporarily for varying periods of time—anywhere from one week to an entire month. While thousands of students who reside in residence halls around the country struggle with the challenges of homelessness during breaks, the hurdles to attend a college or university begin well before most homeless students step foot on a college campus.

A month before his 18th birthday, Jeffrey Williams found himself homeless, like many emancipated foster youths. Williams had no way to properly prepare for being on his own at such a young age. Knowing a college education would be his way out of homelessness, he focused on applying for financial aid, which proved to be more difficult than he expected. Williams needed to prove he was independent with no family to pay his bills to receive financial assistance. Unfortunately, this burden of proof fell on Williams, who, like most homeless students, did not have access to the necessary paperwork. Despite eventually winning his appeal with his school and being recognized as an independent student, Williams still received most of his financial support in the form of student loans. He graduated from college with $44,000 of student loan debt, more than $10,000 more than the national average (Kasperkevic, 2014). Williams's experience is not unique, as most homeless students have difficulty completing the FAFSA because of their inability to access information on their parents' income and assets or obtain a parent's signature (Dukes, Bowman, & Lee, 2013). Although Williams was able to manage his college debt and graduate, often homeless students become overwhelmed by not only the cost of higher education but also the distress caused by their homelessness.

Like Jeffrey Williams, Danae Vachata struggled to prove her status as an independent student. At one point, she even printed out her bank statements for the previous three years and highlighted every expense she had to prove to her university that she was not spending money on things she did not need. In reflecting on her experiences as a homeless student, Vachata admitted, "Your 'state of mind' is greatly influenced by your surroundings and is difficult to zone out the heavy, negative influences that are abundant in the lower socioeconomic atmospheres" (Kasperkevic, 2014, para. 28). The distress caused by homelessness is not only physical but also emotional. As Vachata points out, homelessness can often result in a variety of mental health issues and often is accompanied by another unmet basic need: food.

Acute Risk: Food Scarcity in Higher Education

In his third year at Georgetown University, Paul Vaughn decided to move off campus to save money. He also chose not to purchase the basic campus meal plan, assuming that buying his own food would be cheaper and easier. However, it was not long before Vaughn had trouble budgeting $50 a week for food, and he had to work two jobs to pay for his meals (Bahrampour, 2014). Experiences like *food insecurity*, defined by the Department of Agriculture as lack of "access . . . to enough food for an active, healthy life" (Resnikoff, 2014b, para. 10), are not typically associated with students in higher education; however, this has been a steadily growing population. Although it is difficult to track the definitive number of students experiencing food insecurity, a report titled "Hunger in America" (2014) estimates that about 10% of its 46.5 million adult clients are currently students, about two million of whom attend school full-time. Nearly one third of those surveyed also reported they had to choose between paying for food and covering educational expenses within the last year (Resnikoff, 2014b).

"Between paying rent, paying utilities and then trying to buy food, that's where we see the most insecurity because that's the most flexible," said Monica Gray, director of programs at the College Success Foundation–District of Columbia (Bahrampour, 2014, para. 5). In fact, a 2014 University of Oregon survey (Cancel-Tirado, Lopez-Cevallos, Patton-Lopez, & Vazquez, 2014) found that 59% of students at Western Oregon University had recently experienced food insecurity; in 2009, 21% of students at the University of Hawaii at Manoa reported having been in the same situation (Bahrampour, 2014). Although this is a growing issue on college campuses, students experiencing food insecurity often have few options in acquiring healthy food. Most full-time students do not qualify for food stamps unless they are the sole supporters of a child younger than 12 (Bahrampour, 2014). Even for those students who do qualify, very few on-campus vendors accept food stamps as payment.

Yvonne Montoya, who returned to college in 2012, knows this struggle all too well. "I know what it's like to . . . have a full-service cafeteria in front of me and not be able to access it because they're not accepting food stamps" (Resnikoff, 2014a, para. 2). Although Montoya qualified for food stamps, she often went hungry on campus because the mid-size Los Angeles County institution where she took classes did not have any locations that accepted food stamps and there was nowhere nearby to use them (Resnikoff, 2014a). Another student stated,

> Almost as bad as the hunger itself is the stress that you're going to be hungry. . . . I spent more time thinking how am I going to make some money so I can go eat, . . . and I focus on that when I should be doing homework or studying for a test. (Bahrampour, 2014)

Consumed with the anxiety of not knowing how or where he would be getting his next meal, this student describes the stress caused by food insecurity, which had a direct impact on his ability to succeed academically.

Other college students who experienced food insecurity shared similar experiences, such as emotional distress because of going to bed hungry or feelings of being physically weak because of not eating (Bahrampour, 2014). One student posted on a Facebook confessions page that she was monetarily helping to support her family, so she only had a five-meal-per-week plan, which meant she was "'REALLY REALLY hungry all the time.'" She also confessed to having suicidal thoughts, prompting other students to offer her their meal plans (Bahrampour, 2014).

Success Strategies to Effectively Serve Low-Income Students

As can easily be seen, food insecurity, homelessness, and their accompanying stress have a tremendous impact on the health and wellness of our college students. According to the National College Health Assessment data set, 33.3% of college students rated finances as either "traumatic or very difficult to handle" (American College Health Association, 2013, p. 15). Furthermore, for this and a variety of other reasons, 42.3% of college students stated that they were under "more than average" stress, and 10.4% stated that their stress level was "tremendous" (American College Health Association, 2013, p. 16). Despite the challenges low-income students face in entering college and persisting to degree attainment, our society still positions higher education as the gateway to success. Statistics support this position. As shown in Figure 8.1, earning potential substantially increases with degree attainment.

Collegiate enrollment management staff members often note that access without the proper support systems and environments to create success can be a cruel joke for college students. Thus, we need to move beyond simply increasing access to higher education for low-income students by accepting them into our institutions and offering them opportunities to accumulate debt as a way to cover the cost of tuition. We need to cultivate communities, systems, and policies that engender their success. The following three examples of success strategies can be implemented at any institution that strives to serve low-income students.

Success strategy 1: Economic distress task force. An economic distress task force (EDT) is the first and perhaps most pivotal step your campus community can take to provide the very best services to economically disadvantaged students. Most higher education institutions are so compartmentalized and

Figure 8.1 Annual income by educational attainment.

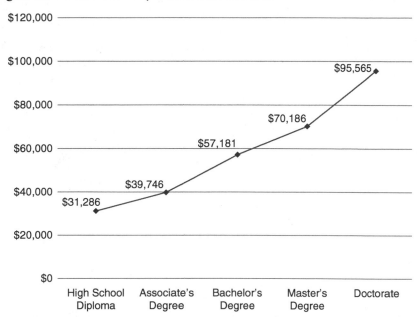

From *Color by Number: Understanding Racism Through Facts and Stats on Children*, p. 94, by A. Munin, 2012, Sterling VA: Stylus. Copyright 2012 by Stylus Publishing. Reprinted with permission.

have so many moving parts that an EDT is the only way to fully view the scope of financial distress on your campus and identify options that are available to mitigate it. In addition, the EDT can assist in creating institution-wide acceptance, enabling you to cultivate services that truly engender student success.

Leadership for this group should include staff who provide a wide range of services in your institution, paired with a degree of institutional authority. We recommend that the dean of students office sponsor your EDT, with an assistant or associate dean acting as its chair or leader. The dean should be present throughout the year, attending several meetings and supporting its mission. However, since this group must be ready to respond to emerging student issues, its management should be led by a staff member who is closer to the front line of student services, allowing the group to be nimbler.

You should consider your EDT group's membership carefully. Service to students who are economically disadvantaged is appealing to many higher education professionals, so an open call for such a task force may be met with an overwhelmingly positive response. Although this is laudable, an EDT group that is too large can inhibit the task force's functionality, and if its members do not have the ability to affect larger systems, it ultimately will not enable positive change at your institution. For this reason, we suggest that your EDT group membership be composed of individuals who not only care about and are concerned for economically disadvantaged students but also have positional authority to bring direct benefits to students. The following offices have staff who could benefit your EDT:

- dean of students
- financial aid
- student accounts/bursar
- federal TRIO program student support services
- university counseling services
- multicultural student success/diversity advocacy
- housing services
- student affairs budget manager

Again, we recommend including staff from the assistant or associate director level from these departments in your EDT group. These staff members should work diligently to keep their supervisors informed and, should the need arise, call on the directors or deans of their offices for additional support.

In convening a first EDT meeting, we recommend asking all participants to come prepared to discuss their experiences with economically disadvantaged students at your institution for comparison with the experience of students on your campus and the national picture of higher education. The goal of this discussion is to move the group toward understanding the economic issues experienced by students at your institution from a systemwide perspective. Participants must understand that, while they are at the table because of their individual expertise, for an EDT to truly be successful the membership needs to view these economic issues holistically and systemically. Some groups may find it helpful to end this conversation by drafting a mission statement.

Moving forward, the meeting structure and scheduling may vary depending on your campus. During the school year, monthly meetings work well at most institutions because they allow the group to form a cohesive bond over time and grow accustomed to identifying collaborative solutions to complex student issues. Meeting monthly also allows group members to learn the yearly work flow of each unit, particularly when each area gets busy and why.

This information allows the members to learn how students experience an institution, and it gives members a break from their silos.

As for structure, an EDT meeting can be broken into three parts. The first part, announcements, is an opportunity for each department to highlight programs, office changes, or personnel shifts pertinent to the EDT and provides a good time to check in on how each staff member is doing. This first part is often the time when the greatest amount of collegiality is built and, therefore, should not be undervalued. The second part of the meeting can move in a couple of different directions. For some meetings, you could invite an EDT member or a guest to make a presentation on topics that affect the work of the EDT, such as

- enrollment, retention, and student success data and trends;
- developments in federal financial aid programs;
- changes in tuition discount rates or institutional financial aid awards;
- student employment;
- student housing cost projections;
- tuition increases; and
- changing student demographics nationally and locally.

Instead of a presentation, the second part of a meeting could be a group discussion on a pertinent student issue. For instance, several years ago an EDT group discussed a change in the cost of textbooks for introductory mathematics courses. Previously, the use of a textbook for the course gave rise to a secondary market of inexpensive used books that helped students with limited funds. However, the department moved to an online text that could only be purchased by a single student and could not be passed on to any other student. As a result, many students could not obtain the textbook and were ultimately unsuccessful in the course. Although the EDT group was not able to alter the curricular plans of the department in question, it was able to construct a strategy for providing emergency funding to low-income students so they could purchase the online textbook.

The third part of the meeting could focus on a discussion of individual students who are experiencing economic difficulties ranging from homelessness to unsustainable debt, allowing a coordinated response to help students and preventing overlapping departmental efforts. EDT members can be tasked with pulling financial aid records, calling shelters, seeking housing accommodations on campus, or other actions depending on the student's emerging need. For these conversations, the EDT needs members who have the ability to access information and make informed decisions to assist students. Additionally, this discussion alerts all parties involved and can prevent students from shopping problems around different departments and receiving more aid than they need.

As the academic year progresses, the leader of the EDT should review the notes from the conversations that occur during the third part of the group's meetings to identify trends. If any exist, a discussion during the second part of a future meeting will be warranted. Overall, this meeting structure addresses EDT group cohesiveness, enables staff to grapple with larger trends and financial realities, and addresses the individual needs of students in economic distress.

Furthermore, we recommend that your EDT leadership host an open campus student economic summit once a year. This is an opportunity for administrators from across your institution to learn about the current economic state of your students. The knowledge you gain at this event will be invaluable as you seek to broaden the group of allies and advocates in your university community. Additionally, these summits can bring to light new issues or struggles previously not identified by your EDT. After all, even the smallest higher education institutions are complex, and communication across departments can be challenging. Such summits can bring forth meaningful information that might otherwise be difficult to disseminate.

Finally, every three years your EDT should reassess its mission, scope, membership, and work outcomes. The terrain for our economically disadvantaged students is constantly changing, so you must commit to periodic reevaluation to ensure that your EDT members are aware of and responding to the contemporary issues on your campus.

Success strategy 2: Emergency funding. Many campuses offer emergency funding for students who confront sudden economic need. Whether the crisis is because of a fire, theft, a parent losing a job, or as simple as broken glasses, institutions must be poised to respond. After all, as has been demonstrated, many of our college students do not have the familial economic support to weather a tragedy or loss in a way that does not affect their academic success. As we have heard from administrators from across the United States, many students are one car accident, tragedy, theft, or loss away from having their academic journey come to a halt. Ultimately, we cannot prevent a tragedy, but we can help smooth out any aftereffects.

First, with any student emergency funding plan, a policy must be created that reflects not only the mission and values of your institution but also the funds you have available. The following questions must be answered when creating this policy:

- Which students are eligible to receive emergency funding? Are they
  - undergraduate or graduate students?
  - full or part-time students?
  - enrolled in an online programs and live in a completely different geographic area?
  - non-degree-seeking students?
  - students who are also full-time employees of the institution?
- How many times in an academic year or career can a student receive emergency funding?
- What is the financial limit of assistance?
- What are allowable expenses among the following that can be covered in emergency assistance?
  - tuition
  - books
  - housing (rent, utilities)
  - food
  - care for dependents
  - transportation
  - legal fees
- Will you be required to notify your financial aid office of this award? If so, how could this financial assistance affect a student's financial aid award?
- What paperwork will you require? What documentation will you require to substantiate the economic need?

Second, you should determine who will administer this policy and provide this assistance to students. We highly recommend designating one office in general and one employee in particular for these tasks. The dean of students office is likely best situated to assess these cases in close communication with other office staff in financial aid, student accounts, and housing services. The dean of students staff member best positioned to oversee this policy is the professional charged with running the EDT. In addition, EDT members should be kept up to date on any trends in student emergency funding requests.

Third, regarding the source of the student emergency funding, we hope your institution will be able to annually allocate resources to provide this service to students; however, this does not need to be the only source of funding. Consult the fund-raising arm of your institution to identify donors who may be sympathetic to this initiative and formally request a gift from them to provide this additional funding. Be aware, however, that such a grant may come with strings attached. A donor who generously offers funding may also specifically stipulate how the funding will be allocated. Another funding source is your university's employees. Many institutions allow their employees to make donations using their paycheck before taxes are withheld, and they often allow their employees to choose the initiatives they wish to support financially. Setting up your student emergency assistance fund as a pool for employee donations can be a big financial win for your endeavor. Finally, throughout the year, but especially in November and December, many department staffs work together to support charitable endeavors. For example, one year a division at an institution allowed employees to wear jeans to work one day in December if they made a donation to the student emergency assistance fund. This charitable event generated more than $3,500 in one day. A similar event at your institution can not only help fund your emergency assistance fund but also bring staff across campus together to support some of its most vulnerable students.

Whatever form your student emergency funding program takes, it can have a substantial impact on the persistence of your students, but you should be forewarned of possible consequences. Once faculty and staff at your institution learn about this initiative, two things will inevitably happen. First, they will refer students to the professional running this program, telling them that the dean of students office has emergency funding available, and if they go to the office they will get a check. Second, once students hear of this funding source, you may be inundated with inappropriate requests. Be prepared to say no more often than you say yes. Declining requests can be difficult. Many students who may genuinely be in need still may not qualify for assistance. These programs start with the best of intentions, but to successfully run them, the administrator often needs a very thick skin.

Success strategy 3: Student food pantry. As food insecurity can be a present yet invisible problem for many college students, more institutions across the country are grappling with this issue head-on by creating student food pantries on campus. However, before you dive into putting together bags of groceries, you should take several steps.

The most difficult task will be conducting an institutional needs analysis. This is the process of collecting information to identify which students at your institution are struggling with food insecurity. Unfortunately, data on this population are scarce, but through your EDT and other campus stakeholders, you can compile anecdotal information. If this process uncovers student stories and experiences exemplifying the plight of food insecurity at your institution, it is safe for you to assume that many others are in similar life circumstances operating below your radar. Unfortunately, you may not truly start to understand your institution's full need until services start being offered, and students walk through the door.

Next, you should undertake an assessment of community resources, including documenting the local food pantries, their hours, and whether they are accessible for your students. Depending on what resources are available in your community, it may not be necessary to create a pantry on your campus. Your work may be to promote the local food pantry and to direct students toward it. Of course, we highly recommend working with the food pantry so it can be prepared for an increase in demand.

Another viable option is to contact a local food pantry to find out if it could extend its services to food-insecure students. In many ways, this is the best option for a university because it creates a resource for students and frees administrators from day-to-day management of a food bank. Administrators at a large private university in Chicago used this method to begin a student food pantry. An assistant dean of students formed a partnership with a nearby food pantry to distribute bags of groceries to students each Tuesday from 10:30 a.m. to 1:00 p.m. In its first year (2011–2012), this partnership served 60 students; the following year, the pantry served 93 students, a more than 50% growth rate.

If a partnership with a local food pantry is not possible for your institution, you will need to decide whether you are willing and able to run an independent food pantry. Your institution's community and government relations office should be able to tell you what, if any, permits or municipal permissions are necessary. Then, space must be identified and staffed appropriately. It is a sizable endeavor to organize food delivery and distribution, so we dissuade anyone from believing that it can simply be added on to one professional's regular duties. Running a fully functioning food pantry is a full-time job, with support still needed from many other stakeholders and volunteers. Another significant consideration in running a food pantry is its availability when classes are not in session. If your institution closes down operations at certain times of the year, you will need to develop a contingency plan for the students who rely on the bag of groceries your pantry provides.

Additionally, regardless of how your food pantry takes shape, there is an educational opportunity. At the previously mentioned large private university, its wellness office regularly worked with the student food pantry by providing educational resources on nutrition. This information was added to every bag, along with information on how to contact office staff to ask for more resources or to seek advice related to health and wellness. Consider how you can encourage students to use the other services provided by your institution that will help them gain knowledge and skills that will ultimately help them escape food insecurity.

Finally, as you develop your plans for implementing a student food pantry, we highly recommend contacting the College and University Food Bank Alliance (www.cufba.org), formed by the Michigan State Student Food Bank and the Oregon State University Food Pantry to assist higher education institutions across the country in providing resources for the food insecure and alleviate the hunger experienced by far too many college students. As stated on its website, "CUFBA was started to support both existing and emerging campus food banks, so please join up and take advantage of being able to connect with the other member institutions. . . . Take what you need, and leave what you know." The group's resources include student interview forms, charts on how best to distribute food, and new client welcome handouts. More than 190 institutions associated with this organization offer support and resources at a range of higher education institutions across the United States.

Assessment: How Do You Know It Works?

We caution any professional from assessing the value of services for low-income students based solely upon retention percentages. Although it is absolutely essential to work to retain students, surviving is not the same as thriving. A piece of quantitative data may indicate that a student was retained, but it says nothing on the quality of that student's experience. In assessing these services we relied heavily on collecting student stories and sharing them with staff throughout the institution. These stories are often hidden, and bringing them forward offered an invaluable lens through which to view the student body. In many instances, these stories served as a catalyst to discuss health care coverage availability, student worker jobs and pay, institutional office hours, times and locations of campus events, and the creation of new positions such as an assistant dean of students for case management.

In addition, strong retention numbers benefit the institution, but continuing at an institution may not be in the best interest of the student. It is heartbreaking, but sometimes the best course of action is to take a break from school or transfer to another institution that can better meet the student's needs. Again, when this occurred we used the details of the student's plight in discussions with colleagues to determine how changes could be made in the future to avoid seeing a student's journey at our institution end in such a manner. Such work assisted in efforts to redesign how financial aid packaging information was shared with new students and their families.

The final piece of assessment that is perpetually ongoing is evaluating what else the institution can do to assist low-income students. Ten years ago, many of us would not have imagined that we would be running food pantries on campus. What services will we be running a decade down the road that we have not envisioned yet? This can only be answered through the diligent work and creative problem solving of dedicated higher education professionals.

In grappling with these exceedingly difficult assessment questions, we highly recommend for all student affairs professionals to read and employ the self-assessment tool published by the Lumina Foundation titled *Beyond Financial Aid* (Chaplot, Cooper, Johnstone, & Karandjeff, 2015). This self-assessment guide gives higher education professionals an opportunity to engage in dialogue throughout the institution and ask critical questions on the gaps in support for low-income college students.

Conclusion

In conclusion, as you and your team begin this substantive and multi-faceted work, remember that Rome was not built in a day. True, this is a cliché, but it is accurate for this endeavor. For the majority of institutions, fostering success for low-income students in a specific and targeted fashion is a brand new initiative. The champions in this arena will need to focus on this work as if they were running a marathon, making slow but steady progress over a long period of time. Change does not come overnight; this work entails creativity, tenacity, passion, and commitment to success over the long term.

The story of Jacob, a low-income college student struggling through homelessness and food insecurity while juggling papers and tests, was not related to provide an example; he is a real student who was served by the success strategies in this chapter. A plan was developed to assist him through an EDT, which allowed us to coordinate services and cut down on his getting bounced from office to office seeking help. Jacob was also able to access emergency funding at the institution, which helped with the purchase of textbooks and some personal items. Some might believe that for a person in Jacob's shoes any amount of financial help would be met with joy; however, that is not necessarily the case. His situation was analogous to being sick, going to the doctor, and being told that although resources are available, you are only going to receive 30% of what you need. These were difficult conversations because Jacob's needs were greater than the allotted funding. Finally, Jacob was a regular recipient of groceries from the student food pantry, which cut down on his food costs, allowing him to use funds elsewhere. It is important to note that despite these concerted efforts to ensure Jacob's success, this story cannot be wrapped up in a pretty bow. Jacob is still struggling. However, Jacob is also still here, and that is plenty enough reason for hope. This work is not and will not be easy, but we can push for success in the continued struggle.

Action Items

For any administrator interested in increasing support for low-income students and enabling their success, we recommend the following:

1. Make data your friend. You need to immerse yourself in the demographic, financial, retention, and success data for your institution. All higher education institutions are required to compile such information. If you have difficulty locating the data at your school, see the National Center for Education Statistics (nces.ed.gov/globallocator). This search tool provides information on tuition, financial aid awards, applications, enrollment, retention, graduation, and loan default rates.
2. Compile community resources. It is impossible for an institution to meet the needs of all students all the time. Familiarize yourself with the community resources outside your institution. Additionally, once the resource list is compiled, develop an online presence so students can access the list any time of the day or night.
3. Build a coalition. Whether through an EDT or another entity, this work cannot be handled by a single person or department. True success will only be achieved when a collective across the school is invested in fostering success for low-income students.

References

American College Health Association. (2013). *National college health assessment: Reference group executive summary fall 2013*. Hanover, MD: Author.

Aries, E., & Seider, M. (2005). The interactive relationship between class identity and the college experience: The case of lower income students. *Qualitative Sociology, 28,* 419–443.

Aud, S., Wilkinson-Flicker, S., Kristapovich, P., Rathbun, A., Wang, X., Zhang, J., . . . Dziuba, A. (2013). *The condition of education 2013*. Washington, DC: Government Printing Office.

Bahrampour, T. (2014). More college students battle hunger as education and living costs rise. *Washington Post.* Retrieved from www.washingtonpost.com/local/more-college-students-battle-hunger-as-education-and-living-costs-rise/2014/04/09/60208db6-bb63-11e3-9a05-c739f29ccb08_story.html

Baxter, A., & Britton, C. (2001). Risk, identity and change: Becoming a mature student. *International Students in Sociology of Education, 11*(1), 87–104.

Cancel-Tirado, D., Lopez-Cevallos, D., Patton-Lopez, M. & Vazquez, L. (2014). Prevalence and correlates of food insecurity among students attending a midsize rural university in Oregon. *Journal of Nutrition Education and Behavior, 46*(3), 209–214. Retrieved from: http://hdl.handle.net/1957/45177

Chaplot, P., Cooper, D., Johnstone, R., & Karandjeff, K. (2015). *Beyond financial aid: How colleges can strengthen the financial stability of low-income students and improve student outcomes.* Retrieved from www.luminafoundation.org/beyond-financial-aid

Cortes, C., & Munin, A. (2014). *Homeless in higher education: The marginalized and invisible.* Retrieved from www.iacac.org/2014/homeless-higher-education-marginalized-invisible

Cruz, J. L., Engle, J., & Lynch, M. (2011). *Priced out: How the wrong financial-aid policies hurt low-income students.* Retrieved from edtrust.org/resource/priced-out-how-the-wrong-financial-aid-policies-hurt-low-income-students

Dukes, C., Bowman, D., & Lee, C. (2013). *College access and success for students experiencing homelessness: A toolkit for educators and services providers.* Greensboro, NC: National Association for the Education of Homeless Children and Youth.

Engle, J., & Tinto, V. (2008). *Moving beyond access: College success for low-income, first-generation students.* Retrieved from files.eric.ed.gov/fulltext/ED504448.pdf

Gross, L. (2013). *College campuses see rise in homeless students.* Retrieved from www.usatoday.com/story/news/nation/2013/10/21/homeless-students-american-colleges/3144383

Hunger in America. (2014). Retrieved from www.feedingamerica.org/hunger-in-america/our-research/hunger-in-america/

Increasing college opportunity for low-income students. (2014). Retrieved from www.luminafoundation.org/resources/increasing-college-opportunity-for-low-income-students

Kasperkevic, J. (2014). Homeless college students and the fight to escape poverty through education. *Guardian.* Retrieved from www.theguardian.com/money/2014/jun/08/homeless-college-students-poverty-education-family-home

Korn, M. (2015, February 3). Big gap in college graduation rates for rich and poor, study finds. *Wall Street Journal.* Retrieved from www.wsj.com/articles/big-gap-in-college-graduation-rates-for-rich-and-poor-study-finds-1422997677

Martinez Tucker, S. (2014). Getting more low-income students into college isn't about money, it's about the curriculum. *Forbes.* Retrieved from www.forbes.com/sites/realspin/2014/03/04/getting-more-low-income-students-into-college-isnt-about-money-its-about-the-curriculum

Maslow, A. H. (1943). A theory of human motivation. *Psychological Review, 50*(4), 370.

McCollum, S. (2014). *How predatory college loans are bankrupting the financial future of America's youth*. Retrieved from www.alternet.org/education/how-predatory-college-loans-are-bankrupting-financial-future-americas-youth?page=0%2C1& paging=off&current_page=1#bookmark

Munin, A. (2012). *Color by number: Understanding racism through facts and stats on children*. Sterling, VA: Stylus.

Resnikoff, N. (2014a). *How one student is fighting the college hunger crisis*. Retrieved from www.msnbc.com/msnbc/the-hunger-crisis-americas-universities

Resnikoff, N. (2014b). *The hunger crisis in America's universities*. Retrieved from www.msnbc.com/msnbc/the-hunger-crisis-americas-universities

CONCLUSION

Tying It All Together

Vijay Pendakur

In the summer of 2015, around the time I was drafting this conclusion, I was invited to testify in Washington, DC, at a hearing conducted by the U.S. Commission on Civil Rights.[1] With the impending reauthorization of the Higher Education Act, created in 1965, the commission members were interested in gathering expert testimony on the experience of minorities in higher education, focusing on strategies and interventions that result in increased access as well as greater collegiate success. Over the course of two days of expert panels, the commissioners listened to testimonies and asked questions to understand the current terrain of risk and success, along with opportunities for the federal government to more effectively contribute to programs that bolster minority students' yearly persistence and timely graduation. While I was deeply appreciative of the commission's interest in increasing access and success for students of color, I couldn't help but notice the way the conversation carefully skirted questions of identity as a factor in persistence and timely graduation. Race needs to be at the center of any productive examination of the collegiate experience of students of color. In the panel of witnesses of which I was part, some of the panelists tried to bring a sense of race consciousness into the dialogue, but the overall conversation never dealt with the core questions of how racial identity might be contributing to risk and success on our campuses. To be clear, I mean not only the subordinated identities of the minority students of color on which the commission was focused but also the centrality of Whiteness in higher education as a normative campus culture and a potential barrier to meaningful inclusion and student success.

Flying home, I reflected on the hearing and found myself disappointed but not surprised at the shape of the dialogue. Retention and student success in higher education is a national concern, but identity consciousness remains tucked away in the margins of public discourse. My experience with the U.S. Commission on Civil Rights only deepened my conviction that books like this one are sorely needed right now to expand the discourse so that identity, including race, can be meaningfully incorporated into the strategies and interventions we employ in the years to come. As noted in the introduction to this book, the national movement for student success has produced an overall improvement in four- and six-year graduation rates at a wide variety of institutions. At the same time, graduation rates for minorities and low-income students have not improved at the rate necessary to close the opportunity gap, resulting in relatively stubborn differences between these marginalized groups and their more privileged peers (Brusi, Cruz, Engle, & Yeado, 2012). If we are going to accelerate the success of students of color and low-income students at our institutions, the programmatic interventions offered in the chapters of this book must be successfully implemented on our campuses. This conclusion covers a number of strategies for institutional change to involve your campus in cultivating student success for all students, including ways to set an agenda for change by making strategic use of institutional data.

Paving the Way: Strategies to Foment Institutional Change

As many higher education professionals have learned the hard way, just because you have brilliant ideas and powerful strategies doesn't mean you can successfully implement them in your campus context. The barriers to successful institutional change are many and all too familiar. Rather than focus on detailing the barriers, I thought it important to offer a number of techniques I've found to be effective in creating the conditions necessary for the programs in this book to be properly implemented. The first part of this section represents a case study in how one institution approached systemic change to promote overall student success. The second part of this section is focused on how one can use data to create a compelling case for institutional change.

California State University, Fullerton: A Case Study in Successful Institutional Change

Most colleges and universities have a five- or six-year strategic plan for institutional change. And these days, most strategic plans include one goal that touches on some form of student success. Rarely, however, does an institution make the success of all its students a singular, cross-cutting agenda. At my institution, California State University, Fullerton (CSUF), this bold choice has already demonstrated significant positive results.

Beginning in 2012 with the selection of a new university president, CSUF embarked on an ambitious strategic planning process that named the following as one of five key goals for the institution between 2013 and 2018: "Improve student persistence, increase graduation rates University wide, and narrow the achievement gap for underrepresented students." ("Strategic Planning," n.d.). While this alone isn't unusual, the ambitious goal becomes clearer in the stated objectives tied to the goal. CSUF defined success for this goal with the following measurable objectives:

- Increase the overall six-year graduation rate so the fall 2012 cohort of first-time full-time freshman is at least 10 percentage points higher than that of the fall 2006 cohort.
- Increase the four-year transfer graduation rate so the fall 2014 cohort is at least 10 percentage points higher than that of the fall 2008 cohort.
- Reduce by at least half the current 12% achievement gap between underrepresented and non-underrepresented students.
- Increase participation in high-impact practices (HIPs) and ensure that 75% of CSUF students participate in at least two HIPs by graduation. ("Strategic Planning: Goal 2," n.d.)

These bold metrics offered a high bar for institutional transformation, as universities are rarely able to shift their overall graduation rates by 10 percentage points during the life cycle of a single strategic plan, let alone close the extant opportunity gap by half in that same time frame. As of July 2015, our institutional research and analytical studies office reported that CSFU is on target to meet and exceed these objectives. The key to attaining these dramatic outcomes at CSUF lies in the strategic approach to sharing ownership and accountability and reenvisioning resources.

Sharing ownership and accountability. Rather than electing a retention czar, CSUF developed a shared ownership of the retention strategic plan by employing a college-based approach to institutional change. Administrators of each of our nine academic colleges were asked to create a student success team (SST) to manage their college's campaigns to improve yearly persistence rates, overall graduation rates, and close the opportunity gap. The SSTs represent a true collaboration because every team has an associate dean (faculty leader), an assistant dean (student affairs specialist housed in the college), a college career specialist (student affairs or career center staff member assigned to the college), a retention specialist (academic advising staff member for underclassmen), and a graduation specialist (academic advising staff member for upperclassmen). Being a public institution with a lean budgetary model, CSUF had to collaborate with its students to impose a student success fee, which the students decided how to appropriate through a consultative process with the administration. The money from this fee paid for the college career specialists, the retention specialists, and the graduation specialists for each of the nine SSTs.

By empowering the academic colleges by putting them at the center of the retention strategic plan, CSUF is able to conduct retention and graduation campaigns that reach the students in the central place where they experience college life at a commuter institution: their curricular experience. Since risk and success are not confined to curricular matters, the SSTs represent a constellation of resources and approaches from across campus: faculty leadership, student affairs and career expertise, and academic advising methodology. Each SST is required to propose campaigns to improve yearly retention rates and overall graduation rates, for its college, as well as closing-the-gap plans for the college's underrepresented minority students.[2] Each college is accountable for its own plan, which is far more manageable than having one overall institutional retention or closing-the-gap plan.

The SST concept is particularly effective at large, diverse institutions that have dramatic differences in student risk and success among the academic colleges. A key feature of the SST concept that allows for success in large, diverse institutions is the SST Steering Committee, composed of the chair of each college-based SST, the director of the career center, the director of the central academic advising center, the provost, the vice president for student affairs, and two associate vice presidents who manage the operations and logistics of the Steering Committee. Every month, the Steering Committee meets to manage accountability for the overall institutional retention and graduation goals and to raise and address any issues that have surfaced at the college level. Because the Steering Committee manages overall institutional accountability, the varied efforts of each college-based SST are kept on track with the institutional strategic plan. At the same time, each college-based SST has its own operational agenda and local approach to increasing student success based on its unique ecosystem. This balance between localized operational tactics with centrally managed strategy and accountability creates a powerful partnership for changing the campus ecosystem to promote student success.

Reenvisioning resources. Retention and student success initiatives can be extremely labor intensive. In today's national budgetary climate, continually requesting more staff to work on these issues is probably not a successful strategy. At CSUF we were able to form partnerships with students to collect the Student Success Fee to support growing staff roles, a number of which contribute directly to the retention strategic plan. But it was also critical for us to think beyond staffing resources and take an innovative approach to incorporating technologies that change the way students, staff, and faculty experience CSUF so that each stakeholder can be more effective. In the first three years of the strategic plan period, the Division of Information Technology was a key partner in the retention strategic plan. The following is a list of key technological investments CSUF made to dramatically improve systems and environments to promote overall student success. (Because of the countless proprietary technologies in the marketplace that accomplish similar tasks, I describe what each technology does in general rather than name a specific software package.)

Software for students:

- Mobile-ready, degree-planning tools allow students to map out their degree pathway along with the required courses they need to take ahead of time so that course registration becomes less chaotic and random. Academic advisers can log into the back end of the tool to see what their students have selected before meeting with them for an advising appointment.
- Course planning tools allow students to build a sophisticated online schedule around their other personal obligations. Students can enter their work hours, organizational commitments, family commitments, and so on to display in a weekly calendar schedule. Then they can select the courses they want to take, and the course planning software shows them the combinations of courses and sections that will allow them to put together the academic schedule they want while maintaining their other personal commitments. This sophisticated schedule planning tool, embedded in the course registration system, works well with the multiple overlapping commitments today's college students often have to juggle while pursuing their education.

Software for advisers, staff, and faculty:

- Student success electronic dashboards generate real-time data visualizations of commonly queried student success variables in an academic department, college, or program. Faculty and staff can use dashboards to track progress on various student success metrics over time, generate sophisticated reports, and highlight areas of concern for future attention.
- Academic advising software allows advisers (staff or faculty) to run complex, real-time queries against their student lists to compile specific groups for targeted intervention. By simply using the mouse and toggling fields on and off, an adviser can produce a spreadsheet of students that fit a certain set of metrics. For example, an adviser can produce a list of Latino students in the college of business who have earned more than 60 credits but have less than a 2.5 grade point average (GPA) and have dropped an average of one class per semester. This sophisticated querying capability

allows staff and faculty to run nuanced campaigns so students who might not have received timely attention are engaged, supported, and able to persist through to graduation.

- Predictive analytics software mines dozens of data points to indicate specific students who might be at risk, even though their GPAs are in good standing. By empowering advising staff and members of the SSTs with a predictive analytics tool, academic advisers can focus their valuable time on students they may not normally have been aware of or concerned about, or students who may be at risk but are not on academic probation.

Although we might not always think of technology when we plan for resource requests to support retention and student success efforts, countless technologies can empower students to take better control of how they navigate their collegiate experience. Similarly, a myriad of software packages are available that change key staff and faculty capabilities to assess risk, successfully intervene, and manage their time most effectively. By reenvisioning resources that support student success, CSUF has been able to do more with less and achieve powerful results while living in the reality of tight budgets.

Retention and graduation work can be laborious, and it can be hard to tell if your efforts are having an effect. After all, your impact on a freshmen class in terms of graduation rates is not measurable for at least four years, if not more. However, as the result of the intensive strategic approach at CSUF, we do have some early indicators of success. As of summer 2015, our six-year graduation rate for first-time, full-time freshmen is now 62.3%. When the strategic plan was initiated in 2013, the six-year rate was 51%. Moving the needle by more than 10 percentage points in three academic years is a strong sign that our approach of shared ownership and accountability—along with savvy, innovative resource allocation—is producing an inspiring outcome. One possible cause of this shift in six-year graduation rates is the careful attention we paid to not only focusing on the incoming first-year class but also taking a systematic approach to making changes that would affect all undergraduates at CSUF. So students who might have historically finished in six-and-a-half or seven years were the beneficiaries of changes in staffing and technology, thereby allowing them to gain momentum at the end of their journey and finish in six years.

Using Data to Make Compelling Cases for Institutional Change

Every campus in the country that receives federal financial aid is required to report on several key retention metrics in its annual accountability reporting to the U.S. Department of Education. Because of this regulatory requirement, campus administrators are keenly aware of their first-year retention rates and their four- and six-year graduation rates. These numbers are only part of the story, however, and are often not enough, when isolated, to foment a campus-based shift toward a retention and student success campaign. Building a strong partnership with your campus's institutional research staff is critical, as these staff members have access to the raw data that can be mined to tell a much more compelling story about the role of identity and risk at your institution. Rather than only tracking yearly persistence and graduation rates disaggregated by race and gender, a more nuanced set of queries or studies can reveal trends on your campus that can lead to a concerted effort to develop identity-conscious student success programs. The following are examples of ways you can work with your institutional research partners to examine the intersection between identity and student success on your campus.

1. Examine first-year performance, not just persistence: Year 1 to Year 2 retention is a common focal point for many institutional efforts, but it is only a part of the picture. When you drill into your data, you have to first assess meaningful progress rather than simple retention. In the group of students who return for a second year, there is always a subgroup that did not complete enough credits to actually qualify as sophomores. At many institutions, students of color, first-generation students, and low-income students are overrepresented in this underperforming but still persisting group. Unearthing this correlation can put a focus on your campus conversation and stimulate stakeholders to ask the critical question of why some groups are not completing as many credits as others. Because the data you're using are crafted around the idea that identity appears to correlate with risk, the programs and strategies your campus develops to address this serious problem must also be conceptualized using identity-conscious design practices. For example, if you find out that Asian Americans are not completing 30 credits (a full first year at a semester-based institution) at far greater rates than other student groups, the campaign to improve this rate has to be built from inception with the racial and ethnic identity experiences in mind if it is to be an effective campaign.

2. Understand the correlations between first-year academic performance and intersecting student identity characteristics: Once you have a robust campus conversation on student performance, it can be revelatory to examine the intersections between certain risk identities to see if there are pockets of higher risk factors in your student body. Most institution administrators think about race, gender, socioeconomic status, and generation status as individual risk variables, but working with your institutional research staff to chart the performance patterns of students at the intersections

of these identities might reveal outcomes that empower you to develop uniquely effective programs for your topography of risk. For example, if you understand the basic success trends for first-generation students as well as for low-income students at your institution, an intersectional analysis might reveal that mid- to upper-income first-generation students might be achieving stellar GPAs and completing the required number of credits each year. However, their first-generation peers who are also low income might be exhibiting particularly acute risks in their yearly performance. In this hypothetical example, these kinds of nuanced data empower you to build interventions that focus on financial fitness, social capital development, and on-campus hiring campaigns to respond to the possibility that the intersection of generational experience and socioeconomic status produces an acute risk experience on your campus.

3. Pay careful attention to achievers: Institutions tend to focus on failure in their overall retention and graduation planning. Students on probation, students who don't declare majors in a timely manner, and students who fail the weeding-out courses receive a lot of attention. While this might be necessary, it is also critical to study students of color, low-income students, and first-generation college students who are highly successful in our campus contexts. Harper's (2014) analysis of 15 years of academic research and writing on Black male students illustrates the critical elision of stories and strategies of highly successful Black male students in the overall literature:

> The near-exclusive focus on problems plaguing this population inadvertently reinforced a hopeless, deficit-oriented narrative. . . . Few initiatives were grounded in data and perspectives gathered from Black male achievers. Therefore, interventions created to improve Black male student achievement were informed almost exclusively by Black male students who did not succeed in college. (pp. 127–128)

Harris and Harper's (2014) study of successful Black fraternity men, and other studies of successful marginalized college students, challenges us to meaningfully learn from the students who are successful as we seek to empower more students to be achievers. This antideficit mind-set shifts institutions away from questions such as, Why are they dropping out? toward deep inquiry into the mind-sets and strategies of higher-risk students who persist, thrive, and lead on our campuses.

4. Use tools that bypass the deficit trap to unearth the student success challenges at your institution: The assessment tools we use can often shift

the locus of the student success problem back to marginalized students themselves by simply casting them as unprepared, unmotivated, or underresourced. As identity-conscious change agents, it is imperative for us to employ tools that avoid the deficit trap so often found in campus discourse on risk and success. In chapter 7 of this book, Sumun Pendakur highlights one powerful tool, the equity scorecard (Harris & Bensimon, 2007), that can uncover student success challenges on your campus without employing a deficit lens that makes students themselves the problem: "The equity scorecard helps staff and faculty adopt an evidence-based approach to increasing awareness of race-based inequities in higher education as well as developing a sense of responsibility to address the extant gaps" (p. 122). The scorecard builds race-conscious capacities in administrators, faculty, and staff, thereby allowing them to make the reflexive turn of asking what institutional policies, systems, and environmental factors might be creating risk for students of color. Harris and Bensimon's tool is a widely recognized evaluative resource that can galvanize a campus shift toward closing the opportunity gap and investing in identity-conscious strategies along the way.

These four strategies are examples of how you can create nuanced studies on your campuses that unearth valuable data for designing identity-conscious student success interventions. Successful change agents need to be able to move beyond anecdotes toward harnessing local institutional data, along with supportive national research, to make compelling cases for institutional transformation.

Tying It All Together

The concept for this book originated as a simple reflection on the gap between campus diversity efforts and retention efforts. Writing and editing this book spanned a year and a half, and as I worked closely with the amazing people who contributed chapters to this project, I began to see that what began as a focused intervention might have much greater significance for higher education and our nation. Each chapter in this book contains a program model that allows higher education staff and faculty to design an intervention from the ground up with student identities in mind. Every chapter contributes a different strategic approach to retention and student success, and taken in concert, the eight chapters represent a powerful multipronged approach to institutional change. This conclusion addresses big-picture strategic approaches to changing entire campus ecosystems so all students can be successful. Many campuses may not be ready for the specific identity-conscious programmatic interventions proposed in this book. In these cases, change agents must be able to use data to foment a movement for student success at their institutions. Alternatively, institutions that have assigned student success efforts to specific silos or to a retention czar might not experience transformative results because of their fragmented approach. For these institutions, change agents must work to use technology to create coherence across the campus ecosystem while building powerful collaborations for student success among faculty, staff, and the students themselves.

Notes

1. Coverage of this hearing can be found at www.c-span.org/video/?326305-2/ minority-students-higher-education-part-2

2. *Underrepresented minority* is the official term used by the California State University system to refer to Black and Latina/Latino students.

References

Harper, S. R. (2014). (Re)setting the agenda for college men of color: Lessons learned from a 15-year movement to improve Black male student success. In R. A. Williams (Ed.), *Men of color in higher education: New foundations for developing models for success* (pp. 116–143). Sterling, VA: Stylus.

Harris, F., III, & Bensimon, E. M. (2007). The equity scorecard: A collaborative approach to assess and respond to racial/ethnic disparities in student outcomes. *New Directions for Student Services, 120,* 77–84.

Harris F., III, & Harper, S. R. (2014). Beyond bad behaving brothers: Productive performances of masculinities among college fraternity men. *International Journal of Qualitative Studies in Education, 27,* 703–723.

Strategic planning. (n.d.). Retrieved from http://planning.fullerton.edu/

Strategic planning: Goal 2. (n.d.). Retrieved from http://planning.fullerton.edu/ goal2.asp

AFTERWORD

I listened to a radio interview with the chief executive officer of Spirit Airlines, Ben Baldanza, and the interviewer asked Baldanza if the airline gets a lot of complaints from disgruntled customers because the company offers a nontraditional travel experience. Baldanza said yes, like any airline, they get complaints. But Spirit sorts the complaints into two categories: complaints from customers who don't understand what Spirit Airlines actually is and complaints from customers who have an accurate understanding of the company and still had a negative experience. If any of you have traveled, or attempted to travel, with Spirit Airlines, you'll immediately understand this sorting strategy.

Spirit is a no-frills airline that supposedly provides more competitive rates by removing a variety of amenities packaged into the price of a ticket by more traditional airlines. When asked by the host why Spirit chooses to be no frills, Baldanza said that according to economists, airline tickets are considered to be an intermediate good; that is, they are a product or service a customer purchases to acquire another product or experience. In other words, no one travels on airplanes just for the ride; we're all trying to get somewhere. Economists claim that intermediate goods are extremely price sensitive because they are simply a means to an end. In theory, customers would be willing to forego frills for a cheaper ticket because the plane ride is just the time in between leaving your house and starting the thing you are actually trying to do. Spirit Airlines, said Baldanza, is simply trying to operate according to this economic wisdom and survive in the reality of a harsh market.

Whether you're listening to the radio, watching television, or talking with friends at a coffee shop, if higher education enters the conversation, the question of cost is usually right around the corner. We all know the cost of higher education has rapidly outpaced Americans' average annual earnings, accumulated family wealth, and the ability to borrow in the form of student loans. As wide and diverse as the national conversation on the price of college is, buried beneath this discourse is a different and potentially more important conversation. When Americans talk about the cost of higher education, they are also discussing the purpose of higher education, and this is why the discourse of college affordability is so intimately linked to career outcomes and earning potential after college.

There is a growing belief in our society that the purpose of higher education should be more narrowly focused on career outcomes and immediate, postbaccalaureate earning potential. To these ends, institutions have begun to toy with the idea of three-year degrees or reducing the number of humanities credits students are required to take to get a degree. Some states now offer scholarships to students at public four-year institutions who declare a major in science, technology, engineering, or mathematics. Every time I see or hear a news story about how we can streamline college to reduce costs and speed up the time for students to maximize their earning power in the workforce, I think of Spirit Airlines. Is higher education an intermediate good? Is college simply the thing you do between leaving one life stage and successfully landing in the next? Should we respond to increasing market sensitivity by stripping away all the frills of higher education to reduce the cost? Just as the founders of Spirit Airlines had to figure out what their true purpose was to develop their business model, ruminating on intermediate goods challenges me to consider what the purpose of higher education really is, and how we can best achieve this purpose in our current historical context.

Looking back on higher education reveals a number of crucible moments for the American academy, moments when the essence and purpose of higher education were tested by social movements, war, or economic downturns. During these times, it was imperative for us in the academy to not simply have conversations about cost or the best delivery method but to dig deeper into the productive foundation of our institutions to consider the very purpose of what we are trying to do, how we are trying to do it, and for whom we are trying to do it. Considering the past puts this book right at the heart of these critical existential and ontological challenges. We are at the precipice of great change in the American academy. Tectonic shifts in the economy, alongside withering state and federal funding models, have potentially positioned colleges to either radically transform themselves or catastrophically fail. I believe, however, that this crisis can be extraordinarily productive for higher education if we take this as a moment to reexamine our very purpose.

We have an enormous opportunity in front of us. Many demographers predict that by 2020 nearly half the high school graduates in the United States will be students of color. We can observe this trend and do nothing fundamentally different from what we've always done, and students of color and low-income students will continue to face the numerous barriers that emerge from the centrality of Whiteness and elitism in our institutional cultures, systems, and practices. The students who are lucky enough to excel in our colleges and universities might land societally desirable jobs upon graduation and become living anecdotes for American meritocracy. These hard-working strivers might also be used, in a twisted irony, to cast the blame for any differential achievement patterns onto marginalized college students who do not succeed. As dystopic as this rendering might seem, it's not that far off from where we currently are. In this scenario, the purpose of higher education remains intact in its historical legacy: to reinforce the hierarchical mechanisms of a stratified society that privileges a previously dominant culture and prepares students for their ordained positions in the social order.

Alternatively, we can have a much-needed conversation on the purpose of higher education in the context of our present national crisis. If, as a community of educators, we think higher education is a space where multiple constituents of learners and teachers exchange ideas, develop critical communication skills, deepen their emotional intelligence, encounter meaningful difference, and emerge with the tools to be lifelong learners, then we need to attend to the current opportunity to fulfill this purpose for the next generation. I hope this book challenges us to think about *who* our students are and the ways their identities must shape how we structure institutions and programs to empower them for deep learning and student success. It fills me with optimism to know that this book is not a work in isolation and that research and writing on equity, inclusion, and student success is abundant right now. For me, higher education should not be an intermediate good, but we will need a sea change if we are to live our most noble purpose. My hope is that the current crisis provokes us to break from higher education's historical legacy and focus on a new purpose: closing the opportunity gap.

Vijay Pendakur
Fullerton, California

EDITOR AND CONTRIBUTORS

Editor

Vijay Pendakur is currently the associate vice president for student retention at California State University, Fullerton. He is an experienced trainer and facilitator on issues of social justice, diversity, and student success, and has worked with colleges and universities throughout the country. He holds a bachelor's degree in history and East Asian studies from the University of Wisconsin–Madison; a master's degree in U.S. history from the University of California, San Diego; and a doctorate in education from DePaul University.

Contributors

Andrea Arzuaga is currently an assistant director in the Office of Multicultural Student Success at DePaul University. The focus of her work is on the successful transition into the university experience for first-generation college students, low-income college students, and students of color. This encompasses the onboarding experience for students and their families alongside identity-conscious programming, support, and advocacy in the first year. Andrea holds a bachelor's degree in psychology and anthropology with an emphasis on ethnic identity from Cornell College, and a master's degree in educational leadership and policy studies from Iowa State University.

André Bobb is an academic adviser in the College of Liberal Arts and Sciences at the University of Illinois at Chicago. He holds a bachelor's degree in public communication and a master's degree in social and cultural foundations in education from DePaul University.

Jeff Brown is the director of the African American Academic Network at the University of Illinois at Chicago. He is a seasoned higher education professional with experience in retention and persistence services for students of color. He holds a bachelor's degree in political science and a master's degree in education administration and higher education, both from Southern Illinois University.

Michele Enos is the assistant director of social justice education at Northwestern University. She is an experienced trainer and facilitator on issues of identity, inclusion, diversity, social justice, and restorative practices. She holds a bachelor's degree in journalism, with minors in ethnic studies and English from Santa Clara University, and a master's degree in higher education from Loyola University Chicago.

Sara Furr is the director of the Center for Intercultural Programs at DePaul University. Sara has more than 10 years of experience as a social justice educator creating opportunities for students, faculty, staff, and community members to explore topics such as identity development; leadership development theory; and power, privilege, and oppression. She received her bachelor's degree in public policy from the University of North Carolina at Chapel Hill and master's of education in higher education and student affairs from the University of South Carolina. Sara also has a master's degree in liberal studies with an emphasis on urban community development from Loyola University Maryland and is currently pursuing her doctorate in higher education at Loyola University Chicago.

Shaun R. Harper is on the faculty in the Graduate School of Education, Africana Studies, and Gender Studies at the University of Pennsylvania. He is founder and executive director of the Center for the Study of Race and Equity in Education, codirector of RISE for Boys and Men of Color, and an advisory council member of President Barack Obama's My Brother's Keeper Alliance. Harper's research examines race and gender in education, equity trends and racial climates on college campuses, Black and Latino male student success in high school and higher education, and college student engagement. He has authored more than 90 peer-reviewed journal articles and other academic publications.

Eric Mata previously served as an assistant director of postcollege success initiatives in the Office of Multicultural Student Success at DePaul University. He is an experienced trainer and facilitator on issues of social justice, diversity, and male students of color, and has worked with colleges and universities throughout the country. He holds a bachelor's degree in Spanish and a master's degree in college student development and administration from the University of Wisconsin–La Crosse.

Richard P. Morales serves as the director of the Career Planning and Placement Center at Kennedy-King College, one of the City Colleges of Chicago. As part of the College to Career Initiative, he is building the first career services center in the institution's history, using a career discernment and career capital model to help underrepresented community college students achieve success in their careers. His research and practice focus on the sophomore slump in low-income students, first-generation students, and students of color as well as creating a holistic curriculum to help these students make intentional choices about their career aspirations. He holds a bachelor's degree in print journalism from the University of Illinois at Urbana-Champaign and a master's degree in higher education administration from Loyola University Chicago.

Art Munin serves as assistant vice president and dean of students at Illinois State University and is an active diversity and social justice educator. His is the author of *Color by Number: Understanding Racism Through Facts and Stats on Children* (Sterling, VA: Stylus, 2013). He has also been a consultant for higher education institutions, nonprofits, and municipalities all over the country. Munin earned a doctorate in higher education and a master's of education in community counseling at Loyola University Chicago, a master's in multicultural communication at DePaul University, and a bachelor's in psychology from Eastern Illinois University.

Sumun L. Pendakur is the associate dean for institutional diversity at Harvey Mudd College. She is a scholar practitioner as well as a highly skilled facilitator and social justice educator and has worked with colleges, corporations, and organizations across the country to increase capacities for equitable practices and true inclusion. Pendakur holds a bachelor's degree in history and women's studies from Northwestern University, a master's degree in higher education administration from the University of Michigan, and a doctorate in higher education leadership from the University of Southern California.

Tomika Rodriguez is the leadership development training manager at the Athena Center for Leadership Studies at Barnard College. She has served as a diversity educator and trainer, advocate, and facilitator nationally and abroad and has experience in leadership development and training, identity development, and cross-cultural dialogue. She has a bachelor's degree in mass communication from Wright State University and a master's degree in education from North Carolina State University.

Nydia María Stewart is an assistant director in the Office of Multicultural Student Success at DePaul University. She is an experienced presenter and facilitator on topics of social justice, student success, leadership, and identity development. She has a bachelor's degree in communication from the University of Illinois at Urbana-Champaign and a master's degree in higher education and student affairs administration from the University of Vermont.